A Peaceable Pilgrimage

John Fitzgerald

A Peaceable Pilgrimage

Quakers Migration and the Creation of Leesburg, Ohio Highland County, and Southwestern Ohio, 1775–1820

BY JOHN FITZGERALD

Frederick Press
Leesburg, Ohio

ISBN 1-882203-84-4
Copyright 2002 by John Fitzgerald

Additional copies of *A Peaceable Pilgrimage: Quakers Migration and the Creation of Leesburg, Ohio, Highland County, and Southwestern Ohio, 1775–1820,* may be ordered directly from:

John Fitzgerald
149 South St
P.O. Box 393
Leesburg, Ohio 45135

Telephone 937.780.9375 for price and shipping information
E-Mail: jfitzgerald@in-touch.net

Library of Congress Cataloging-in-Publication Data

Fitzgerald, John, 1953-
    A peaceable pilgrimage: Quakers migration and the creation of Leesburg, Ohio, Highland County, and southwestern Ohio, 1775-1820 / by John Fitzgerald.
        p. cm.
    Includes bibliographical references.
        ISBN 1-882203-84-4 (alk. paper)
        1. Leesburg (Ohio)--History. 2. Quakers--Ohio--Leesburg. 3. Ohio--Church history. 4. Society of Friends--Ohio--History. I. Title.

F499.L43 F58 2002
977.1'532--dc21

                                    2002072397

This book is dedicated to
my grandfather, Terry Smith,
and my mother, Rosemary (Smith) Fitzgerald,
who taught me to *follow*
the way of the wandering star.

Acknowledgements

THE WRITING OF THIS BOOK WAS A LABOR OF LOVE. However, the work never would have become complete without the efforts and support of a number of good folk. My thanks to the congregation of the Leesburg Friends Church. The church has been a source of encouragement, and they patiently endured listening to excerpts from the book. The Wednesday evening Bible study group of the Leesburg Friends Church was helpful in reading the early chapters and making suggestions. Peg Simpson, Dudley Cherry, Alice Teeters, and Jim Ellis examined each of the four chapters and added useful comments. Paul Lumbatis, in particular, was invaluable for his constructive corrections to the text. Dr. Jane Brown was instrumental in fueling the creative fires necessary to write the text. Dr. Hugh Barbour was thoughtful in examining the text from the perspective of a scholar. Ina Kelly of the "Quaker Collection" at Wilmington College Library granted wonderful assistance in discovering illustrations and graphs to match the text. Jean Wallis was generous in sharing photos from her collection and making important corrections to the text. Louise McKamey and Mary Jo Cook were able in instructing in the use of a computer to type the manuscript. Marcy Hawley of Orange Frazer Press was a wise guide in aiding the process of publishing a manuscript. Sue Frump willingly took on the tiresome chore of proofreading the text. My gratitude to her for the countless hours devoted to this task.

My wife (Carolyn [Smith] Fitzgerald) and I share a common love of history, religion, and nation. This book flows from the joint dreams we share. I offer it as a gift to our community.

To an open house in the evening,
Home shall men come.
To an older place than Eden.
To a taller town than Rome.
To the end of the way of the wandering star.
To the things that cannot be and that are.

—Author unknown, found in a book of sermons by Henry Sloane Coffin

Contents

Introduction

"(We) propose that the meeting continue to be held at Fairfield
and that there be a house built 76 feet long by 36 ft wide,
the walls to be of brick, to be set on a Stone foundation,
to be raised 12 feet above that, and to be covered
with Joint-Shingles."

—Fairfield Quarterly Meeting, 1822

THE DISCOVERY OF THESE MINUTES eleven years ago launched me upon a journey which resulted in this book. The description above is a plan for what would become the Fairfield Meetinghouse. Construction upon the building began in 1822 and was completed in 1823. The structure stands today much as it was envisioned in the minutes of 1822. It is the oldest existing church building in Highland County, Ohio.

Friends at Fairfield held worship in this house from 1823 until 1912. Friends moved to a new meetinghouse which was constructed in the village of Leesburg in 1912. It is the facility that Leesburg Friends Meeting utilizes as a place of worship today. As Pastor of the Leesburg Friends Meeting, I am strongly interested both in the history of Leesburg and Fairfield Monthly Meetings.

This book is offered as an examination of some of the people, places, and events which influenced the creation of Fairfield Meetinghouse. Local events are placed within the larger context of history and the personalities of that time period. Therefore, this is a study of the creation of Southwestern Ohio and Highland County as much as it is a history of the Fairfield Meetinghouse. In addition, at the end of each chapter, a short section is devoted to current issues. It is my hope that this work will add to our appreciation of the past and allow it to speak to our present moment.

—*John Fitzgerald*
Leesburg, Ohio, 2002

A Peaceable Pilgrimage

Pioneers:

*"(I) have seen with my spiritual eye the seed of Friends
gathered all over this good land and that one day
there will be a greater gathering of Friends here
than any other place in the world."*

—Thomas Beals telling friends in North Carolina
about his visit to the Ohio Country in 1775

IT IS DIFFICULT FOR THE MODERN MIND to grasp that a seafarer upon approaching America in the mid 1700's could detect the fragrance of pine trees about 180 nautical miles from land.[1] Such was the essential freshness of the New World. The Ohio Country of the late 18th century was still a vast wilderness. Virgin forest and unspoiled prairie dominated the landscape which Thomas Beals and party saw in their 1775 visit to the Ohio Country. Indians were present in the area, embarking upon a lifestyle of hunting and gathering. Yet, there were few reminders of the white man's civilization. It was scenes of nature, not buildings put up by man, which were the predominate theme. All of this was to quickly change with the Ordinance of 1787 passed by the Continental Congress. This act would establish the Northwest Territory. White settlers would stream into the area north of the Ohio River to build new homes and claim the dream of the Old World. European immigrants, huddled for generations on land they did not own, came to America with visions of inexpensive land dancing in their collective imaginations. So, the settlers would come. But first there were the pioneers.

QUAKER PIONEERS
IN WORSHIP
DESPITE THE
THREAT OF
VIOLENCE.

THOMAS BEALS WAS AT THE forefront of Quaker migration. To study the life of Thomas and Sarah is to examine the pattern of the Friends spread westward. (It should be noted that "Friends" and "Quakers" are interchangeable terms which will be used throughout this book. Quakers is a nickname for the official religious group called the Religious Society of Friends. Furthermore, Leesburg shall refer to Leesburg, Ohio, and Highland County will mean Highland County, Ohio, in the text)

QUAKERS CAME TO OHIO PRIMARILY FROM VIRGINIA AND NORTH CAROLINA. THOMAS BEALS TOOK THE VIRGINIA ROUTE TO COME TO SOUTHERN OHIO. NATHANIEL POPE FOLLOWED THE TRAILS FROM NORTH CAROLINA TO LEESBURG, OHIO.

Wherever this team traveled, large numbers of Quakers had just arrived or were not far behind.

Beals possessed an extraordinary concern for the Native Americans, therefore many of his pioneer journeys were motivated by his desire to be with the various tribes and share with them in that Spirit whose name is Love. In this expression, he was akin to his contemporary John Woolman (1720–1772). Although John Woolman is rightly remembered for his ministry to Friends in regards to ownership of slaves, he also embarked upon extensive travels to meet with Indians. He ministered to them in the same tender fashion employed by Thomas Beals. Both Beals and Woolman followed in the tradition of William Penn. It was Penn who carved out of the harsh wilderness a "holy experiment" in which European brothers and Native Americans could live side-by-side. It is a remarkable coincidence that Thomas Beals was born the year after William Penn died (1719).

Thomas Beals was born in Chester County, Pennsylvania, (a Quaker center adjoining Philadelphia). He was the son of John and Sarah Beals, formerly Sarah Bowater of an English family of Friends. Thomas had two brothers and four sisters. His brother, Bowater Beals, married Ann Cook, sister of Isaac Cook, who was husband of Charity Cook, a noted Friends minister on the Carolina frontier. From Chester County, John Beals moved his family to Monocacy Carols Manor, Maryland. It was here that his son Thomas married Sarah Ankram. The Beals clan moved on to Hopewell, Virginia. John Beals died in Virginia in 1745, three years before the family moved on to North Carolina.

During this time period Thomas was already making visits to the Indians. He was also engaged in working with new Friends' meetings. Carolina, in particular, was frontier territory during this period. It was ripe for the leavening of Friends' ministry. Beals stopped first at Cane Creek in North Carolina. Then it was on to New Garden where he and his brothers-in-law, Thomas Hunt and Richard Williams, started a thriving meeting. His next move was to Westfield where he helped build up a vigorous meeting. 1753 was the decisive year for Thomas Beals. At the age of thirty-four, and already having been involved in a number of Friends' ministries, he became officially recognized as a minister of the Gospel in that Religious Society. In his latter years, Beals helped to establish a Friends' meeting in Grayson County, Virginia (1793) and was active in Friends' work at Lost Creek, Tennessee (1785).

His most historic journey began in 1775. Accompanied by three younger companions, he began a journey to minister to the Shawnee Nation located in the Ohio Country. A *History of the Friends Church in Leesburg, Ohio* notes that *in 1773, Zebulon Heston and John Parriah were on a mission trip to the Delaware Indians in the Ohio Country.*[2] This would accord them the distinction of being the first Friends on record to journey to the Northwest Territory. Two years later in 1775, Thomas Beals paid a visit to the Shawnee Nation in the Ohio Country. What makes this of historic significance is that Beals was the first Friends minister to come to the Northwest Territory. The 1775 journey for Beals and party (he was accompanied by three other men) would prove to be adventuresome. The trip began with ministry to the Delaware Indians. After visiting with the Delaware Indians and passing a fort not far from Clinch Mountain in Virginia, the party was arrested and taken back to the fort on the charge of being confederates of the hostile Indians. The officers, understanding that one of them was a preacher, required a sermon before they went in for trial. After a period of worship, Thomas shared the Friends understanding of the Gospel and the soldiers were duly impressed.

In fact, one soldier was convinced of the Truth as held by Friends as a result of this sermon. His name was Beverly Milner. Beverly Milner became a Quaker and later moved to the newly established Friends community in

Fairfield (Leesburg), Ohio. He settled near the residence of Sarah Beals and lived in the Fairfield area for the rest of his life. Milner and his descendants became prominent at Hardin's Creek Friends Meeting. He died in 1843 at age 85 and is buried at the Hardin's Creek Cemetery.

Arthur Milner is an ancestor of Beverly Milner and will be 100 years old on June 14, 2002. The son of a Quaker minister (Fremont Milner), he has lived in Leesburg nearly all of his life. The Milner family's coming to Fairfield is the result of the faithfulness of Thomas Beals. The preaching of Beals on the 1775 journey demonstrated his trustworthiness to the soldiers. After the sermon Friends were released to further their journey. They crossed the Ohio River and held many satisfactory meetings with the Indians before returning home safely. Upon coming home, Beals shared with his friends that "*he had seen with his spiritual eye the seed of Friends scattered all over that good land and that one day there would be a greater gathering of Friends there than any other place in the world.*"[3]

In 1778 Thomas Beals once again headed toward the Ohio Country with the intent of ministering to Native Americans. On this occasion he was accompanied by seven or eight other men. The party arrived at the residence of Beverly Milner on the Clinch River where some more Friends joined the group. When they were about to resume their journey, Beals spoke to them and said he could not see the way clear to start again. They re-entered the house and sat in silence for some time. At length Thomas broke the silence and gave them a good sermon. While he was preaching, a squad of horsemen under the command of a Col. Preston drew near the house. Preston informed the party that he would not let them pass to visit hostile Indians. Daniel Scott in his *History of the Early Settlement of Highland County, Ohio*, describes what happened next: *Col. Preston was much pleased with the preaching, as well as the earnest devotion and self-sacrificing spirit manifested by the preacher and his companions. They seemed unconscious of danger, and impressed with the belief that the voice of Christian love and the promised rewards of obedience to the promptings of the inner spirit could not fail in their effects on the hearts of the savages. But Col. Preston knew the Indians better, and advised Beals and his companions to return, which they reluctantly did.*[4]

Thomas Beals was not a man to give up. Two years afterwards, he again led a party into the Ohio Country with the intent of ministering to the Indians in God's love. The group crossed the Ohio River and came to a stream called Bluestone about fifty miles above the falls of the Kanawha. However, after a short stay and for reasons unknown, the party was forced to return home.

The danger of travel among Indians finally caught up with Beals and his party in the spring of 1781. A group of Friends were hunting in the Ohio Country when hostile Indians discovered their camp. The Native Americans awaited the return of the hunting party and upon arrival shot dead five of the men. Two of the men were taken as prisoners. One of the prisoners was James Horton, the son-in-law of Thomas Beals. The prisoners were taken to Old Chillicothe (Frankfort, Ohio) and after being tortured, were burned at the stake.

In 1794 or 95, Thomas Beals, accompanied by Nathaniel Pope, took a journey which would lead the two men to present day Highland County for the very first time. An interesting story is told from this journey which illustrates the hardships and depredation these pioneers experienced. At one point the twosome became lost in the mountains of Virginia. They could not find their way out, growing weak and fatigued with hunger. At length they drew straws, and it fell upon Nathaniel Pope to sacrifice his horse so that they would have something to eat. Pope asked for a half-hour reprieve before he shot the horse. In desperation he hurried to a nearby river to see if by chance there was a duck or goose feeding at the water. Instead, he heard the noise of a canoe, and from a distance he feared it was hostile Indians. As the party drew near, to his great joy he discovered not Indians, but Indian traders. These men furnished Pope and Beals with all the food and ammunition they needed.[5] Beals and Pope reached Highland County by traveling the Ohio River until it reached the Scioto. They traversed the Scioto until it was joined by the Paint Creek Watershed. Following Paint Creek, the two men arrived in the northern part of Highland County. It was this trip which would also lay the groundwork for another venture just one year later. It was this journey which would set the foundation for the establishment of Fairfield meeting.

The party began its journey in 1796. It would take six years to settle what is now Leesburg, Ohio. By this point Thomas Beals was a seasoned veteran of the Ohio Country.

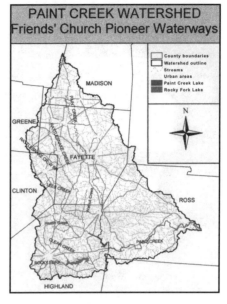

PAINT CREEK WATERSHED
Friends' Church Pioneer Waterways

County boundaries
Watershed outline
Streams
Urban areas
Paint Creek Lake
Rocky Fork Lake

N

MADISON

GREENE

FAYETTE

CLINTON

LEES CREEK

ROSS

CLEAR CREEK

PAINT CREEK

ROCKY FORK

HIGHLAND

THOMAS BEALS
AND NATHANIEL
POPE CAME TO
HIGHLAND COUNTY
BY TRAVELING THE
PAINT CREEK
WATERSHED.

He had led many a journey into this territory. In fact, it had been a little over twenty years since his first adventure to these parts. Beals and Pope had been encouraged by what they had seen in the lands surrounding Paint Creek. It was a fertile land, rich in game, yet suitable for farming. Settlers were streaming into the Ohio territory by this time. However, no white man had laid claim to this attractive land. In their opinion, this would be the perfect spot for Friends to settle. It would be this vision which would guide Pope, Beals, and other Quakers to Fairfield.

JOURNEY TO FAIRFIELD TOWNSHIP (LEESBURG)

NATHANIEL POPE LEFT VIRGINIA[6] in the fall of 1796 headed for the Northwest Territory. He was accompanied by his large family which included two grown sons, their families, and all their possessions. *Highland County Pioneer Sketches & History of the Early Settlement of Highland County, Ohio*, captures some of the flavor of this journey: *The Pope party traveled in covered wagons, had a large drove of cattle, extra horses, chickens, various pets and camping supplies... Pope had constructed a narrow cart, adapted to the mountain track, with ropes attached at each side, ready to be seized whenever necessity required preventing upsetting.*

In this homely vehicle were stored one bed and some bedding, together with the portable articles most prized by the family. The necessary kitchen furniture was packed on horses. Mrs. Pope rode a horse on a pack, and the remainder of the family, consisting of several boys and girls, walked and rode as opportunity offered. Thus equipped, with a rifle on his shoulder and three or four good hunting dogs following with cart, pack-horses and cows with bells on in the rear, the family turned their faces towards the northwest.[7]

With this description one can imagine that the Pope party was slow moving. It would have been difficult to traverse the Appalachian Mountains with little equipment, let alone carrying along all the necessities of family and home. Towards the latter end of November of 1796, the family arrived at the falls of the Great Kanawha. The weather by this time had already turned cold. So, the party decided to winter at the farm of Leonard Maurice who supplied them with shelter and food. Mr. Pope and sons

added to the food supplies with their able hunting skills. It is recorded that in February of the following year, the party also tapped sugar trees, providing tasty treats for the long winter.[8]

During the winter stay, Mr. Pope had fashioned a boat for his family. When spring arrived in 1797, the family set sail in the boat down the Ohio River (with the exception of the livestock who traveled by land). They utilized the waterway until they came to the French Station—Gallipolis. Gallipolis was one of the earliest settlements in the Ohio country (1790). Douglas Hurt reports in his study of Ohio pioneer towns that Gallipolis had a population of ninety-five men and forty-five women in June of 1794.[9] So by 1797, Gallipolis would have been a thriving town by pioneer standards. It was a natural stopping point for many settlers. At Gallipolis the party exchanged bear and coonskins, which they had gathered during the winter, for needed supplies. Following a short stay, the Pope family once again floated down the Ohio River.

Their next destination was a large fertile tract of ground which came to be known as "Quaker Bottom." This was located in present day Lawrence County, opposite the mouth of the Guyandot River and near the contemporary village of Proctersville, Ohio. An interview with the current

Mayor of Proctersville, (Jim Buchanan) indicates that Quaker Bottom is known to locals as a six mile stretch of land which still borders the river to this day.[10] When the Pope party arrived at Quaker Bottom in May of 1797, there were already some Friends gathered there. When Pope and the other Quakers met for worship, Harlow Lindley points out that it was a historic occasion: *So far as can be ascertained, this was where Friends in the Northwest Territory first sat down to hold a Meeting for divine worship.*[11] Quaker Bottom provided a contact point for Friends on the move. Here settlers could become reacquainted and renewed for the journey ahead. There was heavy intermarriage among Friends, and as a group they were communal in nature. As Douglas Hurt rightly notes, one of the characteristics which distinguished Friends from other groups is that *The Quakers usually came in families and groups, rather than as individuals.*[12] There are records of entire Friends meetings moving from Carolina or Virginia to the Ohio Territory. Hence, the emphasis upon community was paramount among Friends as they traveled from the east to the west. Quaker Bottom was one place where community could be found for the weary travelers.

The Pope party had found a temporary home with other Friends at Quaker Bottom in 1797. They decided to tarry awhile and enjoy life with other folks of a similar persuasion. Some of the other Friends who came to the Bottom during this period were John Walter, Thomas Beals, and Obadiah Overman. These settlers with their families formed a good-sized community. One of the more entertaining stories from this era is *that Friends were holding meeting for worship when word came that the floating mill which they had constructed had broken loose from its fastenings and gone off down the river. The meeting was immediately dismissed, and all the active young men dispatched to find the mill. They could not, of course, know when they set out how far they would have to go, or indeed whether they should be able to overhaul it at all. But it was a most indispensable piece of property, and they were resolved to make the effort. They pursued in canoes till they arrived at Hanging Rock, where to their great joy, they found the mill which had been caught and fastened to the Ohio shore by a settler at that point.*[13]

The Pope party lived at Quaker Bottom from 1797 until the fall of 1799. During that time the men would often go on hunting trips. It is recorded that one such forage took them to Symmes Creek and Racoon Creek in the fall of 1798. While there the hunters killed 83 bears, 10 buffaloes, besides deer and turkey in large number.[14]

Nathaniel Pope stayed at the Bottom not only for the

sake of Quaker community, but he was holding out to purchase land at the right time. The Treaty of Greenville signed with the Indians in 1795 had eased the threat of hostility between pioneers and Native Americans. Safety for settlers was no longer an issue. Furthermore, land was being offered for sale at good prices. It was just a matter of waiting for the right piece of land to be sold at the right time. In the fall of 1799, Pope and John Walters with their families prepared to leave Friends on Quaker Bottom. The desire to purchase good land was the motivating factor which pushed the pioneers onward. Historians record that Walters and Pope *sent their wagons, carts, plows, etc. round by the river to Chillicothe, and packed through the woods, driving their cattle and hogs, on a newly made trace from the Scioto to the falls of Paint, where they wintered.*[15]

The next spring (1800) the party cut their way through the woods from the falls of Paint Creek to a place selected by Pope at present day Leesburg. Daniel Scott marks this as the first white settlement in what would become Leesburg, Ohio.[16] Other historians state that this was only a temporary residence and trace the founding of Leesburg to 1802 when Nathaniel Pope, John Walters, and James Howard came to create the first permanent settlement.

The Pope party stayed for a period of time at the campsite (Leesburg) outside the falls of Paint Creek. They returned to the safety of Paint Creek for the winter of 1800-01. In 1801 a company of Quaker pioneers joined the Popes and Walters at the falls of Paint Creek. The group included James Howard, Seth Smith, and Edward Wright. This group of settlers was different than most of the Friends who came either from Virginia or North Carolina to the Ohio Country. This company of pioneers hailed from Tennessee.[17]

When the weather became moderate in 1802, Nathaniel Pope, John Walters, and James Howard moved from the falls of Paint Creek to what had been a campsite in 1800. With this settlement, these three men are credited as the founders of Leesburg. The three men marked where they wanted their cabins to be built by falling a tree. When this task was complete, the three proceeded to work together on building one cabin at a time. *The History of Ross and Highland Counties, Ohio*, informs us that *James Howard's was the first cabin raised, Nathaniel Pope's the second, and John Walters' last.*[18] It is safe to assume that after the cabins were complete, the three large families of the pioneers quickly moved in and the tiny settlement was begun.

There is one other piece of the story of the founding of Leesburg which must be told. The Quaker pioneers, Thomas

THE FALLS OF PAINT CREEK ARE LOCATED TEN MILES SOUTH OF GREENFIELD, OHIO. THEY WERE A GATHERING PLACE FOR FRIENDS PRIOR TO SETTLING AT LEESBURG, OHIO.

form, Thomas formed a new Friends meeting at Salt Creek. His intent was to meet up with Friends who were gathering at the falls on Paint Creek. However, he never made it to the falls.

The horse on which Thomas was riding ran under a stooping tree. Receiving a grave injury, Thomas died within a few hours in the woods on the banks of Salt Creek. A coffin was created for him from the wood of a walnut tree. He was buried in a field near modern Richmondale, Ohio. Thomas was well over 80 years old at the time of his death. A Friends' meeting was established at near-by Londonderry, Ohio. In the 1900's Friends in Londonderry erected a monument to Thomas Beals. The inscription on the monument reads as follows: *Thomas Beals, First Quaker Missionary to the Indians in the Northwest Territory.*[19] Londonderry Friends have a fitting testament to his life:

and Sarah Beals, had come to join Friends at Quaker Bottom on the Ohio River in the late 1790's. It was largely due to the influence of these kindly old saints that meetings for worship were held at this settlement. However, true to the pioneer spirit, the Beals could not stay in one place for very long. In the spring of 1801, Thomas and Sarah moved with some other Friends and settled at Salt Creek near where the present village of Adelphia, Ohio is located. True to

Thomas Beals carried the message of love to his brother man of whatever race or station, and he carried that message through the gateway into the heartland of a great new Republic.[20]

Thomas Beals came close, but he did not make it to the site of what would become Fairfield Meeting. This was left to his wife, Sarah Beals. Throughout her adult life, Sarah Beals had joined Friends on the pioneer trail. Sarah and

THOMAS AND SARAH BEALS WERE THE FIRST FRIENDS MINISTERS TO VISIT THE NORTHWEST TERRITORY. A MEMORIAL FOR THOMAS BEALS IS FOUND AT THE LONDONDERRY (OHIO) FRIENDS CEMETERY.

Thomas, along with their family, had established new Friends' worship meetings wherever they traveled. So, it would be natural for her to heartily endorse the notion of a new Friends' group that was forming outside the falls of Paint Creek (Leesburg). In the fall of 1802, Widow Sarah along with her sons John and Daniel and their families moved from Salt Creek to the new Friends' settlement at Lees Creek. Several other Quaker families moved into the area at this same time. Friends became established both at Lees Creek and Hardin's Creek. It would be hard to calculate the tremendous positive influence of Sarah Beals upon the fledgling Fairfield meeting. Sarah Beals remained active at Fairfield (Leesburg) Friends meeting until her death on July 7, 1813, at the age of 89. She was buried at Fairfield. Her grave is the nearest one to the door of the Meetinghouse—as if even today she beckons individuals to come inside and discover the "still small voice" of the Divine. Jean

THE GRAVE OF
SARAH BEALS
BECKONS VISITORS
TO FAIRFIELD
MEETINGHOUSE
EVEN TODAY.

Wallis instructs us that Sarah Beals *born in 1724, has the distinction of being the oldest person, as to date of birth, to be buried in Highland County with a tombstone inscription.*[21]

DANIEL BOONE—PIONEER ARCHETYPE (1734–1820)

NATHANIEL POPE WAS AN intimate acquaintance of Daniel Boone. Pope had visited with Boone following the 1794/95 trip, which he and Thomas Beals had made to present day Highland County, Ohio. In fact, it was Daniel Boone who encouraged Pope to seek land in that area. Boone claimed that there was beautiful country lying on the waters of the Scioto and Miamis. In many cases according to Boone, the natural beauty of these lands rivaled that of the fabled Kentucky.[22] Contact between these frontiersmen would have been a natural outgrowth of exploration of common land. Besides the shared pioneer mentality, Pope and Boone came from the same religious tradition. Daniel Boone was a birthright Quaker. His grandfather George Boone was a Quaker dissenter. George Boone, who lived in England, heard reports of a sanctuary for Quakers being established in the New World by William Penn. By 1717 George and his family, including three sons, had landed in Philadelphia. In

1720 one of his sons (Squire) married Sarah Morgan. Squire and Sarah Boone moved to an area near Philadelphia (Berks County). Together the couple had eleven children. Their sixth child, a boy named Daniel, was born to Quaker parents on a Berks County farm on November 2, 1734.[23]

Daniel Boone is usually portrayed simply

as a man of the forest and an Indian fighter, but the truth is much more complex. Although Daniel was often engaged in conflict with the Indians, he was also deeply committed to the Native American lifestyle of hunting and the lore of the woods. As David Maurer tells it, *Boone's debt to his Indian neighbors was more than skin deep. They were the masters of the forest and initiated him into the woods–especially concerning the hunt... We often think of European culture as having overwhelmed the Native Americans, but in the realm of the frontier hunter, it* *was quite the opposite. Europeans who lived in this milieu adopted a variety of native customs that formed the basis of a distinct subculture. Other settlers defamed them as "white savages" or "half Indian." From them (the Indians), Boone learned about trapping, tracking, calls, decoys, disguises, and a host of other methods.*[24]

No matter how greatly he was influenced by local Indian culture, Daniel Boone remained deeply committed to the values of white civilization. His belief in private property separated him from the Indians who practiced communal ownership. In fact, many of Boone's pioneer exploits revolved around trying to gain private property for his family. The private ownership of land was the dream which propelled virtually all white settlers to the Northwest Territory. Added to this was the Quaker love of family and community which Maurer credits to Boone's overriding concern for the white man's value system. Although Boone considered himself a Christian, he never was a churchgoer. One could make the case that in his adult years, the Baptist leadings were stronger than the Quaker roots. His brother Squire Boone became a Baptist minister. The Boone family had long since left the Society of Friends after Daniel's early years. A few of the Boone children had married people outside the Quaker faith, and for this transgression, Friends disowned the children. Daniel's mother (Sarah Boone) was the only family member who seemed concerned enough to keep her membership within the Religious Society. Sarah Boone requested and received letters to continue her good standing among Friends.[25]

Like Thomas Beals before him, Daniel Boone lost a family member (son) to hostile Indians. Like Nathaniel Pope, the travels of Daniel Boone brought him to present day Highland County on occasions. In 1777 Daniel was a prisoner of Indians who stopped to rest and hunt near the Seven Caves. The beech tree to which he was tied for safekeeping was identified later by markings and scars.[26] Pope, Beals, and Boone were all pioneers on the American frontier. However, Daniel Boone has become transformed into an American archetype. Daniel Boone will always be symbolic of the American frontier.

BY THE WATERWAYS...

THE FRIENDS WHO CAME TO the Ohio Country in the early 1800's were traveling by the primary mode of transportation. Wagon trains and waterways were the easiest way for large groups of people, possessions, and livestock to travel. The pioneer imagination was always examining new ways to travel by water route. It was this passion that fueled President Thomas Jefferson. Jefferson dreamed of an all-water highway from the Atlantic to the Pacific. He realized that the demands of a growing, young nation would require better waterways, and he hoped that America would rival Europe due to the bodies of water which stemmed from coast to coast. Upon these waters would flow the trade and travel of a commercial empire. However, by the early 1800's, nearly two-thirds of the North American continent remained unexplored. The territory from the Mississippi River to the

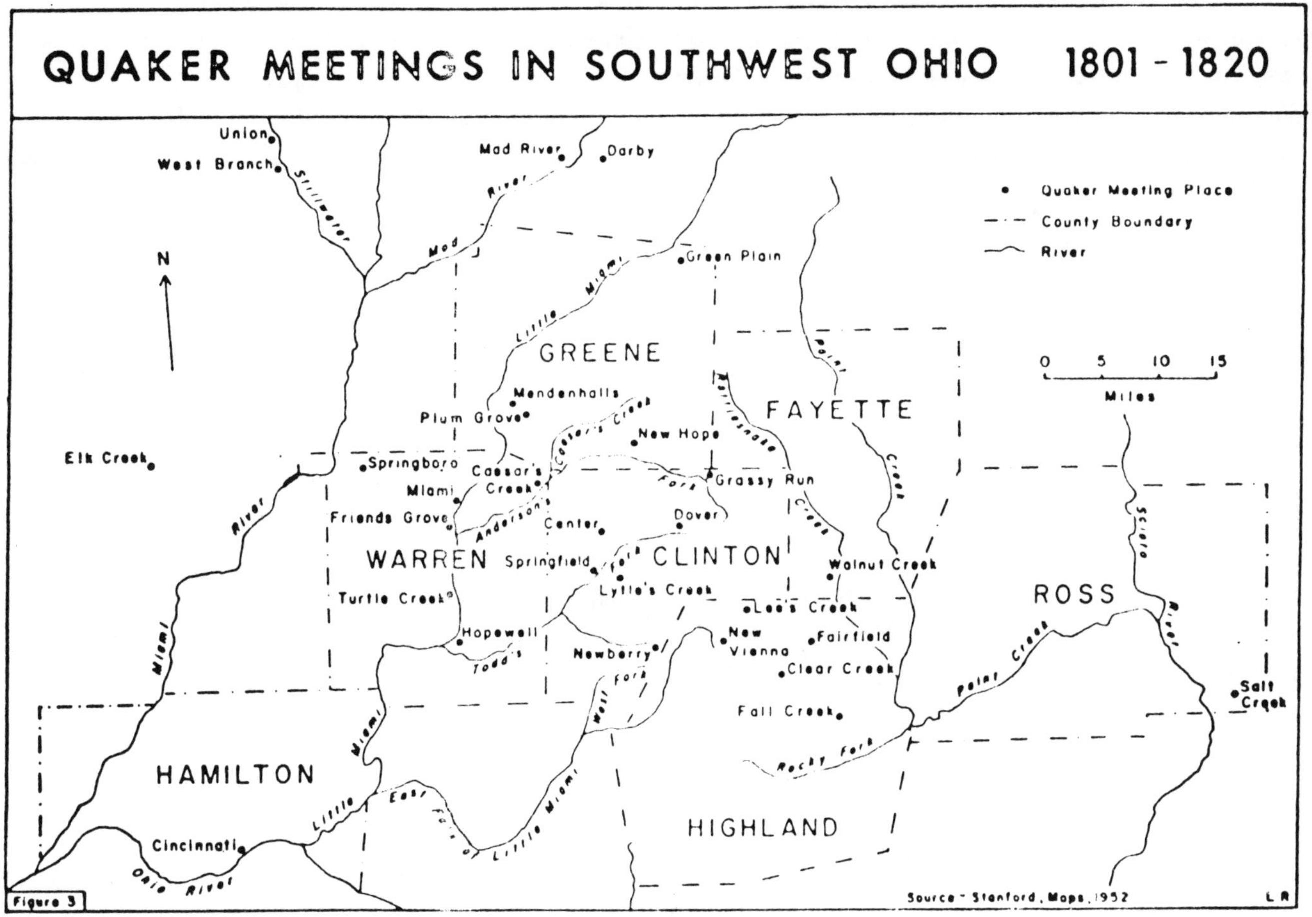

QUAKER MEETINGS IN SOUTHWEST OHIO 1801 - 1820

- Quaker Meeting Place
- · — County Boundary
- ⁓ River

0 5 10 15
Miles

Union
West Branch
Mad River · Darby
Stillwater
Mad River
N
Little Miami
Green Plain
GREENE
Mendenhalls
Plum Grove
FAYETTE
Caesar's Creek
New Hope
Elk Creek
Springboro
Caesar's Creek
Miami
Grassy Run
Fork
Friends Grove
Anderson
Center
Dover
Paint Creek
WARREN
Springfield
CLINTON
Walnut Creek
ROSS
Turtle Creek
Lytle's Creek
Lee's Creek
Scioto River
Hopewell
New Vienna
Fairfield
Salt Creek
Todd's
Newberry
Clear Creek
Miami River
HAMILTON
Fall Creek
Paint Creek
Rocky Fork
East Fork of Little Miami
HIGHLAND
Cincinnati
Ohio River

Figure 3

Source - Stanford, Maps, 1952

L R

FRIENDS ESTABLISHED NUMEROUS MEETINGS IN SOUTHWEST OHIO IN THE EARLY NINETEENTH CENTURY. ABOUT HALF OF THESE MEETINGS REMAIN AS CURRENT PLACES OF WORSHIP.

Pacific Coast had largely been unseen by the eyes of a white man. It was with this thought in mind that Jefferson commissioned two young explorers, Meriwether Lewis and William Clark, who were the ideal choices to lead a team into the uncharted area of America.

Prior to the epoch journey of Lewis & Clark to the land beyond the Mississippi River, a deal had to be made. France held title to most of this land. In the beginning, President Jefferson would have been happy just to purchase New Orleans from the French. No one could conceive that Napoleon would offer to sell the entire Louisiana territory. Napoleon was in a difficult position. He knew that American settlers were already approaching the banks of the Mississippi River. It would be only a matter of time before the settlers would spill across the river over into French territory. There was nothing France could do to reverse this process. Napoleon was occupied with battles in Europe. He could not send soldiers to the New World to defend land. So, he decided to sell nearly two-thirds of a continent for a very small price. Stephen Ambrose puts the matter well: *He (Napoleon) knew what he was giving up and what the United States was getting–and the benefit to France, beyond the money: "The sale assures forever the power of the United States, and I have given England a rival who, sooner or later, will humble her pride."* [27] Final negotiations for the Louisiana Purchase were completed in the summer of 1803. After this, Lewis & Clark would begin their journey.

Thomas Beals, Nathaniel Pope, and Meriwether Lewis were just a few of the thousands of settlers who came down the Ohio River during this time period. While the search for new and better waterways was the motivating factor for Lewis & Clark, the settlers came in search of inexpensive land. The Quakers arrived in a quest for cheap land, and they wanted to live in an area where slavery was illegal. White settlers of all persuasions came to the Ohio Country via the waterways. It is interesting to note that the great majority of Friends' meetings settled in present day Highland County and near-by Clinton County were gathered on streams. Lee's Creek (Fairfield), East Fork (New Vienna), Clear Creek (Samantha), Walnut Creek, Hardin's Creek, and Fall Creek are all Friends settlements which trace their roots to the migration of the early 1800's.

BY THE HIGHWAY...

FOR GENERATIONS THE SHAWNEE Nation trod a footpath across the Ohio Country. In some instances these Indian trails would intersect at villages and then fan out again in different directions. The most common path in the southern Ohio Country was given the name of The Pickawillany Trail. It was different than the white man's journeys since they usually followed the waterways. The Indian thoroughfare began at the confluence of the Ohio and Scioto Rivers (Portsmouth, Ohio). The trail took a northwest direction from there as it meandered towards its final destination of the present day, the Piqua (Pickawillany), Ohio region. In Highland County, Frank Wilcox suggests the Trail *reached Barrett's Mill on the Rocky Fork of Paint Creek; crossing the stream and leaving the knob country, it lifted to the rolling plateau northwest through Rainsboro, then over several tributaries of Rattlesnake, and up the south ridge of Bridgewater Creek to Highland... From Highland the path led northwest over the rolling plateau.*[28] Many of the Indian trails would eventually be transformed by white settlers into highways.

Ebenezer Zane is credited for forming the first major pathway upon which the white man traveled in the Northwest Territory. The Zane family began in America with Robert Zane who came to Philadelphia with William Penn's party in 1682. The Zane clan was endowed with the pioneer spirit and moved frequently to various locations on the American frontier. By the early 1700's, one branch of the Zane family had arrived in Virginia where Ebenezer Zane

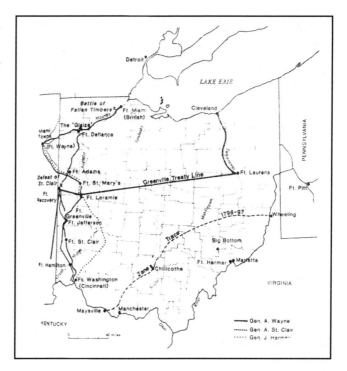

ZANE TRACE WAS THE FIRST MAJOR PATHWAY OPEN FOR TRAVEL IN THE NORTHWEST TERRITORY. SETTLERS STREAMED INTO SOUTHWESTERN OHIO WITH THE CREATION OF THIS ROAD.

was born. Ebenezer Zane, born in 1747, was a grandson of Robert Zane. He married Elizabeth McCulloch, a member of a prominent pioneer family.[29] Ebenezer had the necessary funds to become involved in land speculation. The Zane family pushed westward, eager to obtain new land. In 1770 Zane founded the city where Wheeling, West Virginia, now stands. By 1796 he felt confident enough to petition Congress to carve a wagon road from Wheeling to the Scioto River and then on to Fort Washington (Cincinnati, Ohio), ending at Maysville, Kentucky. Zane persuaded Congress of the cost-effectiveness of a wagon road from Wheeling to Fort Washington, contending that his route would shave 380 miles off the usual 980-mile route from Philadelphia to the military post. Congress approved of the plan, and construction began upon the road which everyone called Zane Trace.

Settlers began to flood into the Ohio Country with the improvement of this major highway. Jean Wallis gives evidence of the kind of population growth which the Zane Trace produced. *In 1797, when the Trace was first being built, George Sample noted two houses on the Trace in the area which included from present day Chillicothe, Ohio to West Union, Ohio. By, 1807, Dr. Fortescue Cuming, traveling from present day Maysville, Kentucky (on the other side of the Ohio River) to Wheeling, West Virginia noted 40 taverns.*[30] If the Zane Trace served the southern Ohio country, it was the National Road which encouraged travel in the central part of the region. Authorized by Congress in 1806, the National Road ran from Cumberland, Maryland, to Wheeling, West Virginia, then across central Ohio, and finally onto Indiana and Illinois.[31] By the time the National Road was built in Ohio, the American frontier had already moved westward into Indiana and Illinois.

Nathaniel Pope and party knew something about the construction of a highway on which settlers could travel. He and his grown sons had constructed a road from the falls of Paint Creek to where Leesburg, Ohio, now stands. It was this pathway which the Quaker settlers traveled in order to reach the new Fairfield Friends Meeting. Pope and party connected their trail with a major road that was being constructed between Chillicothe and Cincinnati, Ohio. The College Township Road began to be cut out of the wilderness in 1797. It began in Chillicothe and passed through Greenfield, Leesburg, Highland and onto Oxford, Ohio. Eventually this road became designated as State Route 28. It was named "College Township Road" because it ended in Oxford, Ohio, where the new state university was built (1809).[32]

With the development of roads and permanent homes, the pioneer era rapidly began to fade. Sarah Beals and Nathaniel Pope were the Quaker pioneers who found their way to Fairfield (Leesburg), Ohio. Beals and Pope paved the way for a new generation of folks that would come to Fairfield. This group would be the Planters, which is the topic of the next chapter.

AMERICA WAS BUILT ON THE PREMISE that anyone can go out into the wilderness and carve out his own fortune. It is part of the "American Dream" to believe that each individual has the capacity to find a better life based upon his own hard work and discovery. It is little wonder that the image of the pioneer has remained a powerful one in the collective psyche of our country. We see ourselves as ever the restless, young explorers. We seek the Promised Land which looms just beyond the next river. Personal freedoms and an individualistic life-style are encouraged as we travel in our journey. Yet, balanced against all of this, is the need for community. Family, church, community, and nation are traditional ways in which Americans have witnessed to the needs of the larger group. Increasingly, we have personal liberties that when expressed do harm to the fabric of the larger group. Consequently, there is always a need for a balance between the pioneer ethic and the building of community. The tension between the two is played out in a number of different ways in contemporary American life. The constitutional freedom of speech which violates the accepted norms of society is one current struggle. The right to seek personal pleasures which threaten the environment is a second challenge.

Perhaps the pioneer Quakers who came to Fairfield had it right. They were individuals, and yet they always traveled within the context of family and community. The personal freedoms were always expressed relative to the greater good of the Meeting.

Sources—

1. Richard Hofstadter, *America at 1750: A Social Portrait*, Vintage Books, New York, New York 1973

2. Lewis Savage, *History of Friends Church in Leesburg, Ohio: A Glorious 150 Years: 1802–1952*, self-published manuscript, page 6

3. Harlow Lindley, *Thomas Beals: First Friends Minister in Ohio*, The Ohio State Archaeological and Historical Quarterly, Vol. LIII, No. 1, January-March, 1944, page 2

4. Daniel Scott, *History of the Early Settlement of Highland County, Ohio*, Southern Ohio Genealogical Society, Hillsboro, Ohio, 1890, page 14

5. Scott, *ibid*, page 21

6. Most histories recount that Pope left from Virginia. Elsie Ayres is the lone exception, telling us that he left from North Carolina. Elsie Johnson Ayres, *Highland County Pioneer Sketches & Family Genealogies*, Hammer Graphics, Inc., Piqua, Ohio, 1971, page 312

7. Ayres, *ibid*, page 313, Scott, *ibid*, page 54

8. Scott, *ibid*, page 54

9. *The Ohio Frontier: Crucible of the Old Northwest, 1720–1830*, Indiana University Press, Bloomington & Indianapolis, 1996, page 193

10. An interview conducted by the author with Jim Buchanan in June of 2001

11. Lindley, *ibid*, page 4

12. Hurt, *ibid*, page 300

13. Scott, *ibid*, page 55 & 56

14. Scott, *ibid*, page 56

15. Scott, *ibid*, page 56

16. Scott, *ibid*, page 56

17. *A History of Ross and Highland Counties, Ohio*, William Bros., 1880, page 397

18. *A History of Ross and Highland Counties, Ohio*, *ibid*, page 397

19. Clayton Terrell, *Quaker Migration to Southwestern Ohio*, self-published manuscript, 1967, page 34

20. Terrell, *ibid*, page 34

21. Jean Wallis, *Times-Gazette* newspaper, Hillsboro, Ohio, January, 1996

22. Scott, *ibid*, pages 20 and 21

23. Michael Lofaro, *The Life and Adventures of Daniel Boone*, The University Press of Kentucky, 1978, page 3

24. David Maurer, *Colonial Homes and Gardens*, June, 1994 pages 83 & 85

25. Lofaro, *ibid*, page 8

26. Violet Morgan, *Folklore of Highland County*, Greenfield Printing, Greenfield, Ohio, 1946, page 26

27. Stephen Ambrose *Undaunted Courage: Meriwether Lewis, Thomas Jefferson, and the Opening of the American West*, Touchstone Book published by Simon & Schuster, New York, NY, 1996, page 101

28. Frank Wilcox, *Ohio Indian Trails*, Kent State University Press, 1933, pages 105–109

29. Ayres, *ibid*, page 16

30. Jean Wallis, *Times Gazette*, newspaper, *Highland Guideposts*,
     March 13, 1997

31. Andrew R. L. Cayton, *Frontier Indiana*, Indiana University Press,
     Bloomington & Indianapolis 1996, page 286

32. Elsie Johnson Ayres, *Hills of Highland*, Hammer Graphics, Inc.,
     Piqua, Ohio, 1971, page 80

CHAPTER TWO

Planters:

Third-generation life in the lower Shenandoah Valley had lost much of its excitement and opportunity; the area's shallow soil, its great distance—both geographically and socially—from the center of political affairs in Virginia, and the inability of its inhabitants to get as fast and as far at they desired were important considerations... To a young man of ambition, the West, with its promises of adventure, wealth, and opportunity, exerted an almost irresistible attraction.

—Thomas Worthington: Father of Ohio Statehood by Alfred Byron Sears

THE PIONEERS WHO CAME TO THE Ohio Country blazed the paths and cleared the forests for others to follow. Unchecked growth quickly became the pattern once the pathways were established and the safety of settlers was no longer a major issue. What had once been a "howling wilderness" was rapidly transformed into cabins and towns with all the trappings of the life left behind in Virginia. Many of the settlers who flooded the southern Ohio Country were transported Virginians. They were women and men of the Shenandoah Valley. They had grown up not as their grandparents who were European immigrants or even as their parents who were colonists of England. They were first-generation Americans who grew up uniquely formed by the values of the Revolution, which had so recently ended in triumph (1783). Now they would turn westward to seek the freedoms and the opportunities which the Revolutionary War had provided.

A study of Fairfield Township in Highland County is indicative of the tremendous migration which took place to this area. When Nathaniel Pope, John Howard, and

AN INDUSTRIOUS POPULATION CAME TO SETTLE THE LAND OF SOUTHWEST OHIO IN THE EARLY 1800'S.

Quaker Meetings in Ohio		
	Meeting Set-off From	Year established
Fairfield	Miami	1804
West Branch	Miami	1805
Elk Creek	Miami	1805
Caesar's Creek	Miami	1805
Center	Miami	1805
Dover	Miami	1805
Turtle Creek	Miami	1806
Union	Miami	1806
Clear Creek	Miami	1806
Fall Creek	Miami	1806
Darby	Miami	1811
Mad River	Miami	1811
Friends Grove	Miami	1812
Cincinnati	Miami	1815
Hopewell	Miami	1817
Springboro	Miami	1818
Harveysburg	Miami	1831
Mendenhall's	Caesar's Creek	1808
Plum Grove	Caesar's Creek	1808
Richland	Caesar's Creek	1822
New Vienna	Clear Creek	1808
Newberry	Clear Creek	1812
Salt Creek	Fall Creek	1808
Lee's Creek	Fall Creek	1817
Walnut Creek	Fairfield	1809
Hardin's Creek	Fairfield	1848
Oak Grove	Fairfield	1861
Springfield	Center	1809
New Hope	Center	1817
Lytle's Creek	Center	1817
Chester	Center	1824
Wilmington	Center	1826
Grassy Run	Dover	1820
West Fork	Newberry	1827
Clarksville	Springfield	1836

Source: David Stanfield, Unpublished document
Figure 5.

Census revealed that already *three hundred and three male inhabitants above the age of twenty-one* lived within the confines of Fairfield Township.[1]

Nathaniel Pope and party were drawn to the Ohio Territory by virtually the same attraction that lured every settler—the affordability of land. The moment of import for Pope came in April through June of 1801. Jean Wallis reports *William Barlow, deputy surveyor for the Virginia Military District, located a survey consisting of 1,016 acres of land for Colonel Richard Clough Anderson... The survey is located in Fairfield Township, Highland County, Southwest and west of the village of Leesburg. Situated today on Survey # 3579 is a section of the village of Leesburg, the Fairfield Quaker cemetery, the Old Brick Meeting house and numerous farms.*[2] It was this tract of land that Pope had been waiting to purchase. His journey to reach this moment had already taken five years. He and his family had waited for two years at Quaker Bottom. The family had been patient while living at the falls of Paint. For an extensive period of time, Pope had been searching for the appropriate tract of land to be purchased at an inexpensive price. While moving to the falls of Paint, Pope had made an agreement with Nathaniel Massie. Massie was a surveyor in the Virginia Military District who had acquired a great deal of land. Pope had sold most of his livestock and

John Walters built their cabins in 1802, they were the first settlers in Fairfield Township. Just five years later in 1807, the first census of Fairfield Township was completed. The corn to Massie in agreement that he would be free to either rent or buy a tract of land at a latter point from him. Nathaniel Massie was a surveyor working under the authority of Colonel Richard Clough Anderson. It would have been natural for Pope to ask for the land which had been surveyed by Massie. This would complete the transaction begun in 1799–1800 when Pope had given Massie much of his personal property. These kinds of arrangements were common for the time period. Douglas Hurt notes that Duncan McArthur, who was another land speculator active in the same area as Nathaniel Massie, rented land in 1801 for *ten bushels of corn and two pounds of sugar per acre.*[3] By 1802 Nathaniel Pope had his land secure and was ready to move to Fairfield Township.

Nathaniel Pope is characteristic of the men and women who moved from being pioneers into folks who became planters. Pope was one of the pioneers who did not move on westward. He settled in Fairfield Township in 1802 and lived the remainder of his years within the boundaries of Highland County. He sowed the first wheat field in the county. He built one of the first cabins. He became one of the first elected officials within the new county. He became established. He was a landowner, a church member, and a respected member of the community. In short, Nathaniel

THE NORTHWEST TERRITORY INCLUDED THE LAND NORTH OF THE OHIO RIVER AND EAST OF THE MISSISSIPPI RIVER.

Pope was representative of the new middle-class America which was brought forth on the frontier. It was the middle-class who shaped and built the small towns and villages that would dot the map of the Northwest Territory. The Northwest Territory would in short order produce five states which would be admitted into the Union. Ohio (1803), Indiana (1816), Illinois (1818), Michigan (1836), and Wisconsin (1848) would form the heart of a great nation. Part of Minnesota would also be included in the territory. It was an immense amount of land. The acreage was larger than most European countries, including England. The Mid-West that these six states comprise would be referred to as the center of middle-class values and morality.

Northwest Territory

A VAST CONTINENT WITH unlimited possibilities loomed westward on the horizon for Americans living in the late 1700's. The lure of land just over the mountains spurred settlers to stream across the Appalachians. Squatters claimed ownership to land with little legal authority to do so. The British government had tried to gain control over the unwieldy spread of pioneers as early as 1763. The Proclamation of 1763 was an edict which prohibited white settlement beyond the continental divide of the Appalachians until officials in London could purchase land from Indians and establish an orderly system for its occupation.[4] It was a plan to direct orderly settlement of the lands between the Ohio and the Mississippi rivers.

However, with limited resources to enforce the proclamation, it soon failed in its mission. By 1774 approximately fifty thousand whites lived on the trans-Appalachian frontier, and the British army could not control them. With the surrender of Lord Cornwallis to George Washington at the Battle of Yorktown in 1781, the success of the American Revolution seemed complete. The 1783 Treaty of Paris made it official. Great Britain ceded its claims to the region south of the Great Lakes. A new nation with immense territory was born. It was a fledgling country shackled with a weak form of government. The United States struggled from 1781 until 1789 under the Articles of Confederation when the Constitution established a new government. The Ordinance of 1787 was by far the most significant act passed by the Continental Congress under the Articles of Confederation. Preparation for the Ordinance took place three years earlier in 1784 when the state of Virginia took a significant step.

Virginia and Connecticut had maintained claims to land on the western frontier following victory in the Revolution. The other states were repulsed by these claims and refused to approve the Articles of Confederation until the land was ceded back to the federal government. After three years of negotiation, the state of Virginia was persuaded to release claims to land north of the Ohio River in 1784. Virginia did, however, maintain a large tract of land called the "Virginia Military District." This acreage was to be used as payment to veterans from Virginia who had fought for the state during the Revolution. The way was now clear for the federal government to take decisive action in regard to the frontier.

The Ordinance of 1787 was a stroke of genius which has had profound ramifications for the building of the United States of America. No less a patriot than Daniel Webster has declared the legislation to be *the most liberty-loving document ever written in history. I doubt, if any law of any lawgiver, ancient or modern, has produced effects of more distinctive and lasting character than the Ordinance of 1787.*[5] At first glance, the Ordinance is simply an attempt to address a political problem. The problem was how to address the squatters and legitimate settlers who were streaming across the Ohio River. The genius came in the principles contained within the Ordinance. Throughout history nations acquiring new lands had generally kept those territories—and their peoples—in an inferior position. It was indeed revolutionary for established states such as Virginia, New York, Pennsylvania and Massachusetts to allow a new territory to join the Union upon equal footing. Once established, this principle set precedent for each new state to become part of the nation. The nation would spread from one end of the continent to the other with each new state having the same status as the original thirteen. Article 5 of the Ordinance of 1787 makes it one of the great documents of American history. The key words are these: whenever *any of the said States shall have 60,000 free inhabitants therein, such State shall be admitted, by its delegates, into the Congress of the United States, on an equal footing with the original States in all respects whatever ...*[6] The second crucial article of the Ordinance is Article 6, which reads: *There shall be neither slavery nor involuntary servitude in the said territory.* The territories of Tennessee and Kentucky had come into the Union, both of them as slave-holding states.

This must have been painful to Quaker pioneers such as Thomas Beals who guided a band of Friends to Lost Creek in Tennessee in 1785. Friends had long held that slavery was an evil that was contrary to the basic teachings of the Christian faith. In fact, the seeds of slavery were so insidious that Friends believed that one could not be a member in good standing and still own slaves. Even a prominent Quaker such as Stephen Hopkins could be read out of meeting for owning a slave. Stephen Hopkins was

Chief Justice of the state of Rhode Island, governor of the state, member of the Continental Congress, and signer of the Declaration of Independence. Despite these impressive credentials, Quakers disowned Hopkins when he refused to grant freedom to a female slave.[7] Such was the seriousness of the Friends' testimony concerning slavery.

Article 6 of the Ordinance of 1787 was a cause for celebration for Quakers such as Thomas Beals and Nathaniel Pope. Here, for the first time in the history of the young nation, a territory was being formed which made it illegal to hold slaves. While it was true that Friends came to Highland County in search of inexpensive land, a second and more primary motivation for them to come to the Ohio Country was the fact that this was the land of the free! The history of Friends' migration was determined by this single postulate. Friends traveled to an area where slavery was outlawed. This meant the Northwest Territory. In droves, Friends came from the slaves states of Tennessee, North Carolina, and Virginia to what would become the free states of Ohio and Indiana.

TO IMPLEMENT THE ORDINANCE OF 1787, Congress would appoint a governor and three judges to administer the territory. When the governor accepted evidence that there were 5,000 free adult males living in the territory, he could authorize the meeting of an elected general assembly and a legislative council elected by the assembly. When a region had 60,000 free inhabitants, Congress could authorize its admission to the Union as a state. It would not take long for the Ohio territory to work through this process. Arthur St. Clair was appointed the first governor of the Northwest Territory in 1788. Just fifteen years later in 1803, Ohio was recognized as a state. During that fifteen year period, the political and social climate of the region was determined by a certain group of young men who hailed from Virginia. These were men who came west eager to find fame and fortune.

The colony of Virginia had been ruled by a small group of planters and lawyers. These men served in the House of Burgesses or on the Governor's Council. Williamsburg was the seat of power. The farmers of the Shenandoah Valley had declined in importance. Alfred Sears, in his study of the life of Thomas Worthington, states well the reasons why the young men of Virginia headed West: *Third-generation* life in the lower Shenandoah Valley had lost much of its excitement and opportunity; the area's shallow soil; its great distance both geographically and socially from the center of affairs in Virginia, and the inability of its inhabitants to get as fast and far as they desired were important considerations... To a young man of ambition, the West, with its promises of adventure, wealth, and opportunity, exerted an almost irresistible attraction.[8]

The Ohio territory offered the promise that would never be found in the gentle hills of the Shenandoah. Nearly all the white men of prominence in early southern Ohio history came from this background of needing to achieve. Back home in Virginia, the symbol of success was the home in which a man lived, a particular carriage, and a certain style of wig and dress which indicated his social standing. Above all else, the confirmation that a man was considered a gentleman was the desired result. Andrew Cayton explains: A gentleman acted the part. He rode his horse well... He attempted to master himself and his emotions. For what earned the "great men" of Virginia deference was their reputation, meaning the public appraisal of behavior... The most famous eighteenth-century Virginian, George Washington, achieved social eminence less because of specific achievements than because of the way he handled himself. Not only did he ride a horse better than any man alive, he was the very model of decorum.[9] It was a certain

unspoken code of behavior. It was a tradition which valued style and ritual over substance. Over a period of time, it would help define differences between North and South and the folks who came to the Ohio territory. The northern part of Ohio was settled by New Englanders. These were Yankee immigrants who had passed through upstate New York and along Lake Erie to reach land that formed the Connecticut Western Reserve. The Yankees who came to northern Ohio were better educated and wealthier than the settlers from Kentucky and Virginia who came to the southern region.[10] Settlers with Appalachian roots dominated the lower south of the territory. These were the country people hailing from the Piedmont, Blue Ridge Mountains, and Shenandoah Valley. They were uplanders from the Virginia Panhandle and Kentucky. New England had a strong tradition of church, the town meeting, and the Village Square. This heritage would be recreated in northern Ohio. The Virginians who came to Ohio were small farmers. They came not with the tradition of the town meeting but rather a certain code of behavior and patterns of conduct that would one day define the meaning of "southern hospitality." A distinct cultural and political difference arose between north and south within the state of Ohio. This difference is manifest even today with Cleveland in the north

CONGRESS
RESERVED SECTION
SIXTEEN NEAR THE
MIDDLE OF EACH
TOWNSHIP FOR THE
USE OF PUBLIC
SCHOOLS.

A Township

6	5	4	3	2	1
7	8	9	10	11	12
18	17	16	15	14	13
19	20	21	22	23	24
30	29	28	27	26	25
31	32	33	34	35	36

of Ohio having a New England flavor in terms of politics and culture, and Cincinnati in the southern part of the state maintaining a Virginian sensibility.

A number of the Virginians who originally came to southern Ohio were young men eager to establish a reputation as "gentlemen." The acquisition of land was the quickest way to solidify one's standing as a man of stature and prominence. The process of obtaining tracts of land was made easy with the passage of the 1785 Land Ordinance. When the state of Virginia ceded its land to the federal government in 1784, Congress passed a Land Ordinance the very next year. Andrew Cayton rightly observes that the purpose of the Land Ordinance of 1785 *was to entice people to buy land; the means was to make land into easily traded commodities.*[11] The idea was to divide the Ohio territory into townships of six miles square, starting at the western border of Pennsylvania. Congress authorized a surveyor from each state to perform the task of outlining the townships. Subdivisions within the townships would be made into one square which contained 640 acres. Each township and section would be numbered to permit easy location by anyone who bought public land. Congress also reserved section 16 in each township to support public education and sections 8, 11, 26, and 29 to meet land bounty claims of Revolutionary War veterans.[12] The setting aside of a township school was the foundation of the public education system which would be so fundamental to the training of American youth. Still today there are vestiges of the one-room school house dotting the countryside. These are the products of the foresight of the Land Ordinance of 1785.

Fairfield Township in Highland County is typical of

the way in which land within the Northwest Territory was divided. Fairfield was one of four original townships which emerged when Highland County was formed in 1805. It was a vast township and when first created, it included more territory than several present counties contain within their boundaries. The four original townships were parceled out to form the seventeen townships that today form Highland County. Fairfield Township currently is comprised of 26,000 well-cultivated acres. Quakers were shrewd in selecting good farm land. It is no accident that the pioneers could say about the land that they were "Fair fields." Friends also selected land where there was a plentiful water supply. Rattlesnake Creek forms the eastern boundary line of the Township. Hardin's Creek winds its way across the southern portion of Fairfield. Clear Creek, Paint Creek, Lee's Creek, Walnut Creek, and Fall Creek all meander in or nearby the present boundaries of Fairfield.

The origins of Highland County also illustrate how land in the Northwest Territory was broken into smaller pieces with the arrival of more settlers. Adams County was the third county established in the State of Ohio. Winthrop Sargent named this huge tract of land after the second President of the United States when it was formed in 1797. Adams County began at Gallipolis on the Ohio

River and extended west until it reached Eagle Creek. The southern boundary of the county was the Ohio River and it went north to present day Delaware County. Ross County was carved out of Adams County in 1798. Highland County stood within the borders of Ross County until 1805. Highland became the twenty-first county to come into being within the state of Ohio when it was formed by an Act of the Legislature on February 18, 1805. As originally constructed, Highland County contained half of the present Fayette County and nearly two-thirds of Clinton County. The county was named because it reminded so many settlers of their Virginia Highlands. When Fayette and Clinton Counties were formed in 1810 and 1813, Highland County was reduced to the way in which it stands today.[13]

VIRGINIA MILITARY DISTRICT

THE SURVEYORS APPOINTED TO DIVIDE the Northwest Territory had a natural advantage. They would know where the good land was to be found and the real value of each parcel of acreage. It is not by chance that quite a number of those who performed the actual survey of the Ohio territory ended up being prominent land

THE VIRGINIA
MILITARY DISTRICT
WAS ONE OF MANY
WAYS IN WHICH
LAND IN OHIO WAS
DIVIDED. THE VMD
IS THE AREA
BETWEEN SCIOTO
AND LITTLE MIAMI
RIVERS.

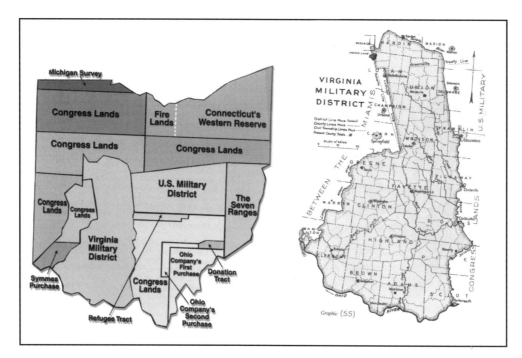

Graphic (SS)

Northwest. At one point Washington had a warrant for 23,333 acres in the Virginia Military District, but he never followed through on the warrant.[14] Washington was a product of the Virginia in which tobacco was the favorite crop for farmers. Tobacco plantations required land and forced labor to perform the hard work. The system of slavery was necessary to maintain the lifestyle that had been developed in aristocratic Virginia. The

holders in the area. This means of obtaining wealth took root very early in the history of our nation. Even the Father of our Nation had desires toward being a large landowner in the new west. George Washington had been a surveyor as a young man in the trans-Appalachian region. Washington knew the value of land and kept a close watch over the territory that was being developed in the

land in the new West would be free of slavery and still afford economic opportunity for those who could afford to purchase large tracts. Land acquired by the surveyors and speculators of the VMD illustrates how these professions could become lucrative. The VMD was 4,204,000 acres of land which had been reserved by Virginia as payment to veterans who had fought in the

Revolution. When Virginia relinquished ownership of land north of the Ohio River in 1784, it held back the land between the Scioto and Little Miami Rivers as a trust for veterans benefits. The only drawback to this trust fund was that the land had scant opportunity to become homes for the veterans. Most of the men were settled east of the mountains and had little desire to move to the wilderness. Thus, most holdings were offered for sale. Speculators and agents were employed to sell the holdings. Surveys were made and abstracts of title prepared. Everyone stood to prosper in this arrangement. The veterans gained a cash settlement. The surveyors, agents, and speculators garnered cash and land. The government had legitimate settlers instead of squatters living on the land. The only real losers were the Native Americans. The story of the Indians in the Northwest is one of unrelieved anguish. It is a spectacle of shame which will be examined in more detail in the next chapter.

By 1800 warrants for practically all the land within the Virginia Military District had been issued. The few remaining parcels of land within the VMD took many years to sort out. In 1871 Congress ceded the stray acres of land to the state of Ohio. Ohio took this land and used it for an endowment for the state university. Thus, Ohio State University benefited from the sell of land within the VMD. However, in 1800, most soldiers instead of coming to live in the territory were content to sell their warrant via a land speculator. This led to a system where surveyors and speculators owned the majority of land within the VMD. In 1800 only seventy-five persons owned a third of the VMD. The largest individual holding was 118,601 acres.[15] The rapid rise of the man who surveyed most of what is now Highland County illustrates this accumulation of land.

Nathaniel Massie started out as an entry clerk in the office of Richard Clough Anderson. In 1793 Colonel Anderson had been appointed surveyor general of the Virginia Military Lands. He had several young men whom he granted the authority to be deputy surveyors. Nathaniel Massie proved to be a capable clerk and surveyor. In 1790 Massie was rewarded by being appointed chief surveyor within the Virginia Military District. In a ten-year period, between 1790–1800, Massie had surveyed the staggering amount of 750,000 acres.[16] Massie quickly became the middleman for the selling and buying of land within the district. One can imagine that the transaction engaged in between Nathaniel Pope and Nathaniel Massie was typical of the time period. In just a few years, Nathaniel Massie

owned 28,400 acres, an area larger than present-day Fairfield Township.[17] Massie had an interesting career with large implications for the entire region. In 1790 Massie established his base of operation for work within the Virginia Military District. He contracted with nineteen other men to form a settlement located one-third of the way between the mouth of the Scioto River and Cincinnati on the Ohio River. This town was called Massie's Station. Later the name was extended to be called Manchester, the first settlement in the VMD and the fourth earliest settlement in the state.[18]

In the spring of 1796, Massie left his settlement on the Ohio River. He took a congregation of Presbyterians with him to build a new village near the mouth of Paint Creek on the Scioto River. Massie was a promoter and knew how to attract settlers. His scheme in the new village on the Scioto was to lay off 456 lots with a promise that the first 100 lots would be given free to settlers. Immigrants flocked to the town and Chillicothe, Ohio, was born. Massie was not only active in land speculation, but highly influential in the politics of the region. Massie, along with his friend Thomas Worthington, led a coalition which worked to move the seat of government to his new village in 1800. It was argued that Chillicothe was at the geographic center of the territory. Therefore, it would serve the area better than a capital located in Cincinnati. The reality was that Chillicothe served the economic interests of men such as Worthington, Massie, and McArthur. Duncan McArthur followed a path similar to Nathaniel Massie. Duncan McArthur worked as a chainman for

Nathaniel Massie. He learned quickly the ropes of the surveyor profession. McArthur was soon involved in the purchase and selling of military warrants with the Virginia Military District. By 1810 McArthur had become one of the four largest landowners within the state of Ohio. He owned 35,341 acres. It is interesting to note that all four of the largest landowners were surveyors and had added to their wealth on the basis of purchases within the Virginia and U.S. military districts and the Western Reserve.[19] McArthur was also prominent in early political affairs. He succeeded William Henry Harrison as Commander of the Army of the Northwest and was elected to serve a term as Governor of Ohio. McArthur also is credited as the founder of Greenfield, Ohio. Greenfield is located in Highland County, ten miles down the road from the Fairfield Meetinghouse. The history of Greenfield begins with a surveying of the College Township Road which the McArthur party was contracted to service in 1796. This road is the modern State Route 28 which runs from Chillicothe to Milford. McArthur purchased the land surrounding the road and marked the trees of the virgin forest where the streets of the town were to be located. The town of Greenfield was laid out in 1799, but the official plat does not appear on records until April 28, 1802.[20]

The life of surveying provided rich rewards. Yet the constant travel under adverse weather took its toll. Nathaniel Massie was only 50 years old when he died in 1813. His body resides under a stately monument in a Chillicothe (Grandview) cemetery. His son, Nathaniel Massie II was a deputy surveyor for over fifty years in Highland County. Duncan McArthur, Nathaniel Massie, and Thomas Worthington all played important roles in the early history of Southern Ohio. The life of Thomas Worthington deserves special attention.

THOMAS WORTHINGTON—FATHER OF OHIO STATEHOOD

WITH THE PASSAGE BY CONGRESS OF the Ordinance of 1787, the Northwest Territory was created. A governor and three judges were given authority by Congress to administer the territory. Governor Arthur St. Clair was given sweeping powers. For nearly a decade he had almost total political, economic, and military power. St. Clair was Commander-in-Chief and appointed all military officers within the militia. Along with the three judges, he adopted laws from the original states to legislate in the territory. St. Clair was also in charge of selling federal lands in the Northwest Territory. It is little wonder that

St. Clair was a Federalist who was interested in keeping power vested in the federal government. The Governor's philosophy is articulated by Douglas Hurt: *St. Clair believed that order must come before liberty and that the frontier people could not be trusted to govern themselves or live peacefully and civilly without firm control and guidance from the territorial government.*[21] Many of the early settlers in the Ohio territory were New Englanders who had a conservative political ideology akin to Governor St. Clair. The change came when the Virginians began to flood the southern and central Scioto valley. The Scioto Virginians favored a Republican form of government. They held that qualified voters in each region should be able to

make political decisions rather than adhering to the actions of the governor. The Republican camp was headed by the new, wealthy landowners of the area. Men such as Edward Tiffin, William Henry Harrison, Duncan McArthur, Nathaniel Massie, and Thomas Worthington joined the Republican movement. Political scrapes took place between the two different schools of thought. The Federalist cause was dealt a blow when the capital was moved to the Scioto stronghold of Chillicothe in 1800. The deal was sealed with the election of Thomas Jefferson to the presidency in 1800. Republicans in Ohio now had a sympathetic voice both in the nation's capital and in the territory. The stage was set for Ohio to become a state. Leading the charge toward statehood was Thomas Worthington of Chillicothe.

Thomas Worthington came from a long line of English and American Quakers. His great-great-grandfather was John Worthington (1606–91) of Cheshire, England. He and Mrs. Worthington (Mabel Owen) were two of the earliest followers of George Fox, founder of the Friends Church. When the Worthington Quakers migrated to America, they faced the same predicament as the family of Daniel Boone. Many of the young people married outside of the Quaker faith. Robert Worthington married outside the Friends Meeting in 1759. Hopewell Friends Meeting promptly disowned the father of Thomas Worthington. Despite this setback, when Thomas Worthington was born in 1773, most of his family members were Quakers and Thomas himself was a Friend throughout his life.[22] Thomas Worthington was representative of the young Virginians who came west to seek a fortune. He had visited the Ohio territory on occasion and spotted land to his liking. He requested that his friend Duncan McArthur survey 7,600 acres for him within the Virginia Military District. With this purchase in hand, Worthington at the age of twenty-five was ready to settle permanently in the new village of Chillicothe in 1798. From this beginning, Thomas launched out and built a land empire built upon purchase of bounty warrants from veterans who owned acreage within the Virginia Military District. By 1800, Thomas Worthington owned 18,273 acres and was well on his way to be among the rich and powerful in the new territory. The Worthington family led the carefree life of gentry which they had known in Virginia. During the years 1805–07, a new home was constructed for the family on a small hill outside of Chillicothe. The home was named "Adena" and it was described as *the most magnificent mansion west of the Alleghenies.*[23] Adena, with its extensive grounds and colonial architectural design, exemplified the tradition of eighteenth-century Virginia aristocracy. The State of Ohio has restored this mansion to its original condition and opened it for public viewing. It remains today a beautiful home.

In keeping with his reputation as a gentleman, Thomas Worthington was open to and respectful of different expressions of the Christian faith. He was at home at

Quaker meetings, camp meetings, and union meetings. While residing in Chillicothe, he regularly attended the Presbyterian and Methodist churches. The famous Methodist bishop Francis Asbury stayed overnight on several occasions at the Worthington home. Worthington's faith was brought to bear on the burning social issues of the day. William Henry Harrison was in favor of the institution of slavery and encouraged Thomas to also grant his support for this cause. Worthington responded that his belief as a Quaker led him to believe that slavery was wrong although he did hire indentured servants.[24] The picture which emerges from these various strands is one of a "gentleman Quaker." Worthington had the piety of a Friend, but his world revolved around the political and economic upper crust of his day. This social standing led him to have a much different witness than Quakers such as Thomas Beals and Nathaniel Pope. Beals and Pope lived in Quaker communities, and the values of Friends permeated every aspect of their lives. In contrast, Worthington did not limit himself to Quaker community and was very much a man of the world.

The economic and social standing of Thomas Worthington did lend itself to political influence. When Worthington arrived in Chillicothe, he became absorbed in the drive towards statehood which was affecting the region. The first territorial assembly met on September 16, 1799. From its inception, the legislature and governor were in conflict. Thomas Worthington was at the forefront in this battle with Arthur St. Clair. The removal of the capital to Chillicothe and the election of President Thomas Jefferson had greatly aided the cause of the Scioto Virginians of which Worthington was a leader. The territory had the required 60,000 free inhabitants necessary for statehood. The only remaining hurdle to cross was establishing the boundaries for the new state. The Federalists desired that the western boundary for the state be set at the Scioto river. This act would reserve power in the eastern Federalist strongholds of Steubenville and Marietta. Worthington and his Jeffersonian supporters favored division of the Northwest Territory at the Great Miami River. The decisive moment came when President Jefferson backed the Worthington coalition and promised that the western boundary for the new state would remain at the Great Miami River. The final battle had been won and Congress passed an Enabling Act for statehood. Ohio became the 17th state to join the Union on March 1, 1803. Thomas Worthington went on to serve as one of Ohio's first two senators. He later became sixth governor of the state. Like Nathaniel Massie, he did not have a long life. His last few years were filled with financial problems and sickness. He died June 20, 1827, at the age of fifty-three and was buried in Chillicothe. There is a Highland County connection to the Worthington family. Thomas had a younger brother named Robert who was born in 1776. Robert followed his older brother to migration in Ross County, Ohio. In 1817 Robert moved his growing family to Fairfield Township of Highland County. Robert Worthington settled on the east bank of Rattlesnake Creek and on Lee's Creek, south of present-day East Monroe, Ohio. The Worthington family remained in this area, and several of the ancestors are buried in the Leesburg (Pleasant Hill) cemetery.[25]

Quaker Planters

IN CHILLICOTHE, WHERE PAINT CREEK joins the Scioto, a new state was being carved out. Just thirty miles to the west, at the headwaters of Paint Creek and Lee's Creek, a new Friends community was being formed. The Friends who came to Fairfield Township in Highland County in 1802 were part of a large scale migration which took place in the area. The influx of settlers to the Ohio territory was dramatic. An examination of the census records indicates the rapid rise in population. In 1800 Ohio had a population of approximately 45,000. By 1810 the state's population had increased to 230,760. By 1820 the total population in the state was 581,434. In 1825 Ohio had a population of approximately 800,000. At this point, it was the fourth most populous state in the Union.[26] In the 1800's, Ohio was destined to become the center of gravity for the nation. It was the link between the older colonial states located on the eastern seaboard and the growing frontier to the west.

Seven Presidents of the United States would emerge from Ohio during this time frame. U.S. Grant was born in Point Pleasant in 1822 and served the nation as the 18th President (1869-77). Rutherford B. Hayes was also born in 1822 in Delaware, Ohio. Hayes became the 19th President of the United States (1877–81). James Garfield was the 20th President to serve our country (1881–81). Garfield was born in 1831 at Orange, Ohio. Benjamin Harrison was a grandson of William Henry Harrison. Harrison became the 23rd President of the United States (1889–93). Benjamin Harrison was born in 1833 at North Bend, Ohio. William McKinley was born in 1843 at Niles, Ohio. He was the 25th President of the United States

(1897–1901). William Howard Taft was born in Cincinnati, Ohio in 1857. Taft was the 27th President of the United States (1909–13). The final President to be born in Ohio was Warren Harding. Harding was the 29th President (1921–23). He was born in 1865 in Blooming Grove. William Henry Harrison was not a native Ohioan. He was born in 1773 at Berkeley Plantation on the James River in Virginia. Harrison was however, very active in early Ohio history. William Henry Harrison was the 9th President of the United States (1841–41).[27]

Quakers traveled to many areas of Ohio besides Highland County. An estimated eight hundred Quaker families had immigrated to Ohio by 1816. There were Friends' settlements in Highland, Ross, Warren, and Lawrence Counties in the southern part of the state. However, the majority of Quakers lived in eastern Ohio, particularly in Belmont, Columbiana, Harrison, and Jefferson counties. By 1827, 8000 Quakers lived in eastern Ohio. A growing center for Friends in eastern Ohio was the village of Mount Pleasant. In 1814 Quakers in Mount Pleasant began the construction of the first permanent Yearly Meeting House west of the Appalachians. Completed in 1815, it seated two thousand Friends.[28] The state of Ohio has helped in the preservation of this building, and it is open to the public. It remains as a testimony to the peaceful ways of Friends. Ohio Yearly Meeting was set off from Baltimore Yearly Meeting in 1813. Sessions for Ohio Yearly Meeting were held in the new facility in Mount Pleasant.

As stated earlier, the pioneer settlement of Friends in Fairfield township was made when Nathaniel Pope, John Walters, and James Howard built their cabins upon the present site of Leesburg in the spring of 1802. It was in 1804 that a small log meeting house was built on the grounds where Fairfield Meeting House now stands. This served as a place of worship for Friends from miles around. The first building was replaced by a second log structure which was much larger. It remained in use until 1822 or 1823 when the brick building which is Fairfield Meeting House was constructed. This build-ing was used for almost a century. It was in 1912

that the present Meeting House was constructed in Leesburg, and in 1916 the name was changed from Fairfield to Leesburg Monthly Meeting of Friends. The formal organization of Fairfield Monthly Meeting took place on July 18, 1807. It was set off from Miami Monthly Meeting of Waynesville, Ohio, by authority of Redstone Quarterly Meeting at Brownsville, Pennsylvania, which was a part of Baltimore Yearly Meeting.[29] Friends in Fairfield had come as pioneers, but they remained settled in the area as

planters. One of the testimonies they witnessed to was peacemakers, which is the subject of the next chapter.

CURRENT ISSUES

THE DESIRE TO CREATE A SECURE dwelling place is a universal need for every human being. The planters came to the Northwest Territory in order to claim land and establish homes. They stayed in the area to plant the political, social, and economic seeds of a vibrant nation. People with strong roots are important to the moral fiber of our country. Far too often our current culture rewards the cult of the individual. What is emphasized is the need to make money and the ability to move from place to place in pursuit of career. Financial gain is important. However, a vital element is sometimes lost in a mobile society. A healthy regard for the larger institutions of society such as family, community, school, church, and country can be broken down in a sea of constant change. Without strong connections to one place, individual mores and values replace the ethics of community. Each man has his own castle, but we must protect it with locks, chains, sophisticated security systems, and even guns. We feel insecure in the threat of violence. The amount of violence which takes place in our homes, schools, workplace, and sporting events is alarming. The mayhem is likely to increase if we continue down the path of pursuing individual liberties without regard to community. The building of community incorporates those rootless folk who slip through the cracks of society. Community disciplines the individual will to submit to the common good. The potential for violence decreases when deep roots are planted.

The Friends who came to Fairfield Township in Highland County taught an important lesson about the construction of community. They came to this area for economic benefit. However, a deeper purpose for their coming was the general welfare of their brothers and sisters. Quakers migrated to Ohio because it was a free territory. Friends could not visualize a community where one woman was free and the other woman was a slave. Genuine community always includes justice and equality.

Sources—

1. Daniel Scott, *History of the Early Settlement of Highland County, Ohio,* Southern Ohio Genealogical Society, Hillsboro, Ohio, 1890, page 146

2. Jean Wallis, weekly *Times-Gazette* newspaper article, *Highland Guideposts,* Hillsboro, Ohio, February 25, 1995

3. R. Douglas Hurt, *The Ohio Frontier: Crucible of the Old Northwest, 1720-1830,* Indiana University Press, Bloomington & Indianapolis, 1996, page 172

4. Andrew R. L. Cayton, *Frontier Indiana,* Indiana University Press, 1996, pages 39-43

5. Clayton Terrell, *Quaker Migration to Southwestern Ohio,* self-published manuscript, 1967, page 10

6. I have borrowed heavily from this resource: Vincent Wilson, Jr., *The Book of Great American Documents: With Inaugural Addresses of Jefferson, Lincoln, Kennedy*, R. R. Donnelley & Sons Company, Crawfordsville, Indiana, 1987, pages 21-25

7. Silas B. Weeks, *New England Quaker Meetinghouses*, Friends United Press, Richmond, Indiana, 2001, page 51

8. Alfred Byron Sears, *Thomas Worthington: Father of Ohio Statehood*, Ohio State University Press, Columbus, Ohio, 1958, page 22

9. Cayton, *ibid*, page 77

10. Hurt, *ibid*, pages 249-250

11. Cayton, *ibid*, page 104

12. Hurt, *ibid*, page 144

13. Wallis, *ibid*, April 3, 1997

14. Tanya West Dean, and W. David Speas, *Along the Ohio Trail: A Short History of Ohio Lands*, The Auditor of State, Jim Petro, Columbus, Ohio, 2001, page 44

15. Sears, *ibid*, page 24

16. Wallis, *ibid*, March, 1995

17. Hurt, *ibid*, page 167

18. Hurt, *ibid*, page 204

19. Hurt, *ibid*, page 176

20. Elsie Johnson Ayers, *Hills of Highland*, Hammer Graphics Inc., Piqua, Ohio, 1971, page 532

21. Hurt, *ibid*, page 274

22. Sears, *ibid*, pages 4-10

23. Sears, *ibid*, page 30

24. Cayton, *ibid*, page 189

25. Elsie Johnson Ayers, *Highland Pioneer Sketches & Family Genealogies*, Hammer Graphics, Inc., Piqua, Ohio, 1971, pages 335-336, 1029

26. Hurt, *ibid*, page 375

27. James B. Cash, *Unsung Heroes*, Orange Frazer Press, Wilmington, Ohio, 1998, pages xi-xii

28. Hurt, *ibid*, pages 299-301

29. Lewis Savage, *History of Friends Church in Leesburg, Ohio: A Glorious 150 Years: 1802-1952*, self-published manuscript, page 10

CHAPTER THREE

Peacemakers:

*Love was the first motion, and thence a concern arose to spend
some time with the Indians, that I might feel and understand
their life and the spirit they live in, if haply I might receive some
instruction from them, or they might be in any degree helped by
my following the leadings of truth among them.*

—The Journal of John Woolman

THE PIONEERS CAME TO EXPLORE the terrain and the waterways of Southern Ohio. The planters who settled the land and established villages quickly followed them. When the pioneers and planters arrived they encountered a native population. The story of the interactions between the Native Americans and the white man is the focus of this chapter.

The Quakers who came to Highland County were symbolic of the unique role Friends were to play as peacemakers between the two competing European and Indian cultures. In fact, the very roots of the Fairfield Friends Meeting of Highland County suggest the powerful way in which Quakers were able to bond with Native Americans. The founding of Fairfield Meeting is credited to Bathsheba Lupton. Lewis Savage tells us, *Bathsheba Lupton had observed that a number of the young men of the settlement were making Sunday visits to the Indian encampments. Under a concern for their moral welfare she rode on horseback from cabin to cabin with her message of exhortation and sometimes stern rebuke which resulted in the*

WILLIAM PENN
INAUGURATED A
LONG LINE OF
PEACEABLE
RELATIONS
BETWEEN QUAKERS
AND NATIVE
AMERICANS

WILLIAM PENN
WAS ONE OF THE
MANY WHITE
SETTLERS WHO
WAS MYSTIFIED BY
THE ORIGINS OF
NATIVE
AMERICANS.

establishment of regular meetings for worship... The first Friends meeting for worship was probably held in the fall of 1802 or early 1803... The Friends gathered on alternate Sundays at John Beal's cabin on Hardin's Creek and at the Lupton's in the Fairfield neighborhood.[1] It is noteworthy that a womon would be recognized as the founder of a local church. Furthermore, it is significant that the initial outreach for worship was made to Friends who were visiting their Indian brothers. In the early years, Friends and Indians were intertwined in activities such as hunting, fishing, and living from the land. The Shawnee had been living in the area for several generations when Quakers matriculated to southern Ohio.

SHAWNEE NATION

THE WHITE MEN WHO CAME TO the shores of the New World were puzzled by the origins of the native population. It was obvious that the Native Americans did not descend from Europe. Stories emerged which attempted to explain the race and background of the inhabitants of the land. One popular notion was that the American Indians were descendants of the lost tribes of Israel. William Penn writing in the late 1600's could write of the Delaware Indians: *For their Original, I am ready to believe* *them of the Jewish Race, I mean, of the stock of the Ten Tribes, and that for the following Reasons; ... they offer their first Fruits, they have a kind of Feast of Tabernacles; they are said to lay their Altar upon twelve Stones.*[2] Joseph Smith would develop this theme a little over a century later. Smith would have a revelation which included a complex theology revolving around the journey of an ancient Israelite prophet Lehi and his family who came to the American continent some 2,000 years ago. The result is the Book of Mormon which proclaimed that the American Indians were the lost tribes of Israel and that the primordial Garden of Eden was located in the United States (Smith later identified the location near Independence, Mo).[3]

Anthropologists have arrived at a far different explanation for the origins of Native Americans. The current theory is that at one time there was a land bridge between the continents of America and Asia. Hunting and gathering tribes could easily migrate from Asia to America. However, the last series of glaciers created a waterway (Bering Strait) that left a gap in the connection between Asia and Alaska. People of Asian descent could no longer return to their ancient homeland. Instead, they became the original inhabitants of the American continent. Archeological evidence suggests that there were humans in Ohio by as early as 13,000 B.C.[4] The modern period for study of Native Americans in Ohio begins with the advent of the Adena culture (900 B.C.–1200 A.D.) The Adena are known for their distinctive burial mounds. Important information was gained about these people from the 1902 excavation of a burial mound. The excavated mound is located on the Adena estate built by Thomas Worthington outside of Chillicothe, Ohio.

Overlapping the Adena period was another group of

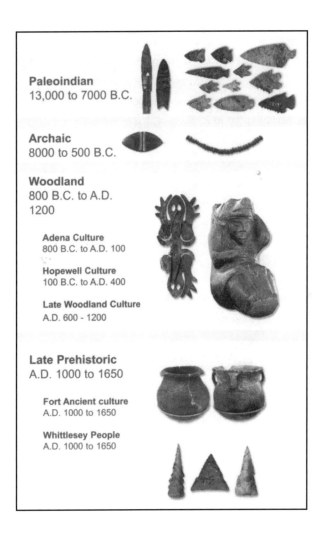

Paleoindian
13,000 to 7000 B.C.

Archaic
8000 to 500 B.C.

Woodland
800 B.C. to A.D. 1200

   Adena Culture
   800 B.C. to A.D. 100

   Hopewell Culture
   100 B.C. to A.D. 400

   Late Woodland Culture
   A.D. 600 - 1200

Late Prehistoric
A.D. 1000 to 1650

   Fort Ancient culture
   A.D. 1000 to 1650

   Whittlesey People
   A.D. 1000 to 1650

THIS TIMELINE DEMONSTRATES THE DIFFERENT PERIODS OF OHIO INDIANS PRIOR TO THE SHAWNEE.

hunters, gatherers, and farmers living in Ohio. The Hopewell people who lived here from 100 B.C. to 600 A.D, built mounds and walls made of earth in geometric shapes: circles, rectangles, and octagons. Fort Ancient in Warren County and Fort Hill in Highland County are testimony to the industriousness of the Hopewell. Indian mounds in Highland County also bear evidence to a former race of people. The Cooper Mound located outside of Leesburg is of particular interest. Cooper Mound is found on a farm in the area of the Fairfield Meetinghouse. The Williams Brothers tell us that when this mound was opened for a second time in 1879, the following discovery was made: *three or four feet of ashes, charcoal, calcined bones and fragments of wood, which, when removed, disclosed a plaster-like substance containing skeletons of five humans, stone tools, ornaments, etc.*[4]

The Adena and Hopewell people disappeared from the Ohio Country for reasons unknown. In 1000 A.D. a new culture centered on Fort Ancient entered the area. The Fort Ancient people were similar to the people in Mexico, like the Aztecs and Mayans. It is conceivable that natives of Mexico migrated to Fort Ancient during this time period. Evidence of the Fort Ancients shows that they were gone by the mid 1600's.

Most anthropologists believe that the Fort Ancient people were the ancestors of the Shawnee.[5] It is little wonder that William Penn, Joseph Smith, and other early settlers were mystified by the background of the natives. Social scientists today debate the origins of the Shawnee Nation. The Shawnee referred to themselves as "sa wanna" which meant "people of the South." Indeed, there is evidence of a fierce band of Shawnee who fought with the Creek and Cherokee Indians in the Deep South. The Suwannee River (of the Stephen Foster song) is named after this nomadic contingent of warriors.[6] Yet at the same time, the Shawnee roamed to the far places of the north. Linguistically linked to the Algonquian, the Shawnee demonstrate ties to the Iroquois confederacy. The Iroquois were centered in New York State, with most of their activity being north and east. Whatever its origin, the Shawnee tribe had established settlements in Pennsylvania by 1692. They lived peacefully with the Quakers until William Penn died in 1718. After this relations with the colonial government began to deteriorate. In 1736 Pennsylvania granted the Iroquois control over all other tribes in the colony because of their military power and partnership in the fur trade. The Iroquois ordered the Shawnee "back toward Ohio, the place from whence you came." The Shawnee were making plans to leave anyway due to white expansion in the area. By 1738 the Shawnee had returned to their ancestral home and established a town at the mouth of the Scioto River (Portsmouth, Ohio). Between the late 1730's and early 1750's the Shawnee had moved into the southern Ohio Country and claimed it as their own.[7]

THE COMING OF THE WHITE MAN

SHORTLY BEFORE THE PERIOD THAT the Shawnee were returning to their Ohio homeland, the French were establishing outposts in Vincennes, (IN) and Detroit, (MI). As early as 1701, the French were constructing the nucleus for an outpost at Detroit. Fur trade was the original attraction for the white man to come to the Northwest Territory. Detroit and Vincennes served as connector points between Canada and Louisiana in the far-flung French Empire of the New World. France never did capitalize upon being the first major European influence in the area. The French had the vision but not the might to build up strength in the new region. In 1749 a military expedition was sent from Montreal to the Ohio River to bolster French claims to an empire. Celron DeBienville led an expedition of 272 men who traveled to various locations in Ohio and left

THIS MAP SHOWS THE LOCATIONS OF MAJOR EARLY INDIAN TRIBES AND THEIR MAJOR TOWNS IN OHIO.

seven lead plates proclaiming the Territory as belonging to France. We know what these plates look like due to the discovery of one of them by two boys who were swimming near Marietta, Ohio.[8] Upon return to Montreal, the army asked for French settlers to come to the Ohio River. The request was made for 10,000 French peasants to come to New France and make their home in the Ohio River Valley.

The request went unheeded. French interests in the Ohio Country soon failed.[9]

British fur traders, by this time, had begun to move into the region. The jousting for the lucrative fur industry between France and England had an effect upon the tribes living in the Northwest Territory. The natives learned to pit one power against the other. The Miami Indians who were partners with the French in the fur industry saw that it was to their advantage to change alliances. The British were coming with large numbers to the region, and the Miami began to do business with them. A contingent of the Miami had traveled from their base in Indiana to build a village in Ohio in 1747. They constructed a town called Pickawillany (which was to become a major Shawnee trail) on the Great Miami River near present-day Piqua, Ohio. In 1752 Charles Langlade led a combined force of French and Indians to punish the settlement for their transgressions of trading with the British. They won the battle but lost the war. It was too little—too late. British traders and pioneers continued to flood the Ohio Country and engage in commerce with the Indians. The tensions in the New World between France and England reached a climax with the outbreak of the French and Indian War (1754-1763). The triumph of the British in 1763 confirmed what was a foregone conclusion. Ohio was a British stronghold. The tide of English immigrants was the key. At the end of the French and Indian War, there were only 125,000 French in all of the Americas. The British colony of Virginia alone was four times as populous.[10] The influx of settlers to the British colonies led to a rapid transformation of the landscape. In the beginning there were a handful of major cities followed by isolated villages located on key rivers and lakes. Everywhere now there was the building of cities, farms, plantations, roads, and homes on the eastern seaboard. In 1700 there were a mere 250,000 people living in the British colonies. By 1750, the population had skyrocketed to nearly two million.[11]

The hunting and gathering culture of the American Indians was being destroyed by the steady spread of the white man's civilization. The Indians moved westward to find new hunting grounds and escape incidents of frontier violence with the white man. The Delaware and the Mingo Indians joined the Shawnee people in the Ohio country in the 1700's. The Delaware were the Lenni Lenape (Common People) whom William Penn encountered while establishing Pennsylvania in the late 1600's. They gained their English name in honor of Lord de la Warr who was one of the colonial governors of Virginia. The Mingos was a name given to Indians who belonged to the Iroquois confederacy. By the mid-eighteenth century, the Mingo had 2,500 people living in villages in northeastern Ohio. Wyandot was an English name for the people the French called the "Huron." The Wyandots came from southern Ontario into the Upper Great Lakes and finally into Ohio perhaps as early as 1738. The Miami tribe came from Wisconsin and had settled into eastern Indiana and western Ohio by the 1740's. The Miami are the lone exception to migrate east to Ohio rather than west.[12] The primary tribe living in southwest Ohio remained the Shawnee. However, the migration patterns remained fluid and there were scattered bands of other tribes who lived in this area. As late as the early 1800's there were Wyandot living with the Shawnee in Highland County. Daniel Scott tells us that a Methodist minister named Edward Chaney preached to a large group of Wyandot on the banks of Clear Creek in 1803-1804: *Mr. Chaney induced them (the Wyandot) to come to his cabin to listen to him preach. They came frequently in large numbers... The Indians did not understand much of what he said but they understood sufficient to satisfy them that it was addressed to them on behalf of the Great Spirit.*[13]

WHILE THE POPULATION OF THE British colonies was growing at a tremendous rate, the American Indians were being decimated by disease brought by the white man. Andrew Cayton shares this sad report: We *do not know how many Native Americans there were in Indiana in the early 1700s. But epidemics in 1715, 1733, and 1752 reduced the population to around 2,000 by mid-century.*[14] The spread of new germs was just one of several ways in which the coming of the white man was to have a profound negative effect on Indian culture. The Europeans did bring new technology that made life more comfortable. The traders came with guns that made hunting easier, and they introduced metal fishhooks to increase the catch. They also took with them iron hoes, axes and knives that eased the hard labor tasks of clearing land and cleaning game. Wool blankets and coats meant women no longer had to depend on animal skins to create warm clothing.[15] However, there was no place to turn to but the white man for repair of broken knives, axes, and other utensils. Furthermore, the Indians became dependent upon traders to supply them with powder for their guns. In short, the new technology would replace the old, but the natives had no means to create and supply the technology on their own. This also meant that with new tools to hunt and trap, the animal population rapidly diminished. The fur trade became oversupplied. Indeed, by the 1760's the fur business in the Ohio Valley was in a state of decline.[16]

The most serious disruption to the Indian way of life by the white man was the introduction of liquor. Liquor and the carrying of new disease were the twin killers Europeans brought to the Ohio Indians. Liquor had a narcotic effect on an increasingly depressed race of people. It was a depressing time. The settlers continued to come to Ohio in relentless numbers. The Americans came in droves in the late 1700's and early 1800's. In just a ten-year period from 1800 to 1810, there were nearly 200,000 white Americans who came to live in Ohio.[17] The onslaught was too much to handle. The rapid changes in lifestyle were too dramatic. The call for annihilation of the Native population on the part of some Americans wrought wholesale fear. Alcohol consumption was considered one way of easing the pain. Liquor became destructive to the fabric of the Indian family and carried with it an increase in the incidents of violence between Indians and whites.

These situations were just part of the general problem of a clash between two different cultures. The Americans and the Indians came from two worlds that were unlike each other. The Americans wanted to clear the forests in Ohio to be used for farming. The Indians viewed farming as the work of women and something demeaning to manhood. The Americans desired to purchase land as a means to obtain wealth in Ohio. The Indians had no comprehension of land sales because private ownership was foreign to their culture. The Americans brought missionaries who preached a new religion in Ohio. The Indians were comfortable with their religious and ceremonial practices that contained a worldview different than the missionaries. The Americans fought wars over land in Ohio. The Indians had a concept of limited warfare that was confined to addressing specific insults or losses. The Americans thought the Indians in Ohio to be weak and inferior because they accepted trinkets and gifts in exchange for territory. The Indians viewed gifts as a necessary building block in the creation of friendship. The exchange of gifts was to be one part of a relationship of mutual friendship and respect. The Americans in Ohio found it a despicable thing for Indians to adopt white captives into their tribes. The Indians viewed adoption of white captives as one way of building their depleted population. The Ohio tribes accepted their adopted children, husbands, and wives as their own.[18] Misunderstandings between the two cultures were unavoidable. It would lead to uneasy tensions and constant violence between the two groups.

The British were the first to advocate the extermination of the native population. Sir Jeffery Amherst, a British Commander-in-Chief of forces in America during the 1700's, had a dislike so strong of the Indians that he proposed giving them blankets infected with smallpox to kill off the population.[19] Other British voices were not nearly as cruel and heartless as the Amherst proposal. Henry Hamilton was the principal British officer in charge of dealing with Indians of the Old Northwest in 1775. Hamilton was interested in the Indian culture and often painted them and romanticized their history.[20] He attempted to portray himself as the Great Father to whom the Indian children must come. This paternalistic attitude conveyed by Hamilton was to be later replicated by American Presidents in their dealings with American Indians. President Thomas Jefferson shared the romantic view of the natives with Hamilton. He believed the Indians could be converted into good farmers. Jefferson had the West in mind as a place where the Indians would find contentment as peaceful tenders of the ground. His speech to the Osage in 1804 indicates both his poetic sentiments for the natives and his firm but simplistic demands as a Father to Children: We *are all now of one family, born in the same land, & bound to live as brothers. The Great Spirit has given you strength, and has given us strength; not that we might hurt one another, but to do each other all the good in our power... You have furs and peltries that we want. . and we have useful things which you want.*[21] Of course, there were those Americans who viewed the Indians as a menace. White settlers living on the frontier and suffering from Indian reprisals of violence desired to see them destroyed. Some white Ohioans agreed with the sentiment that the "only good injun—is a dead injun." There were also whites that attempted to live at peace with the various tribes.

Some of the more daring tales are told about the Quakers and their interactions with the Shawnee Indians when they first moved into Highland County in the early 1800's. Daniel Scott explains that there were Shawnee encampments on the banks of Hardin's Creek when the Friends first arrived. The Indians learned a little English and the two groups engaged in sign language for communication. One day the Pope family was involved in a hunting expedition and chased a bear toward an Indian camp. Scott picks up the story from there: *The Popes were on horseback following the dogs, an*

INDIAN CHIEFS
FROM VARIOUS
TRIBES LED
RESISTANCE
AGAINST THE
WHITE MAN.

Indian met them on foot, gun in hand, and intimated, half by gestures and half by words, that he would like to join in the sport if one of the whites would dismount and thus place himself upon an equal footing with the Indian. William Pope readily accepted the banter, and he and the Shawnee started out on foot... The pair finally reached the place where the dogs had the bear treed and Pope fired first. The bear came down badly wounded, and a desperate fight with the dogs ensued at the foot of the tree. At length the bear caught a favorite dog and was killing him. Pope signed to the Indian, who was nearest, to rush in and tomahawk the bear, but he refused, simply saying "White Man." So Pope rushed into the fight to save his dog, and by bravery and good luck succeeded in tomahawking and knifing the bear until he was dead.[22]

INDIAN RESISTANCE

THE INDIANS IN SOUTHWEST OHIO WERE faced with an inextricable foe in the Americans who came after the opening of the Northwest Territory. There had been earlier uprisings by the natives in response to the coming of the Europeans. In 1762 the Ottawa chief Pontiac led a mixed group of Indians in an attack upon Detroit (which by this time was under British rule). The band had initial success in

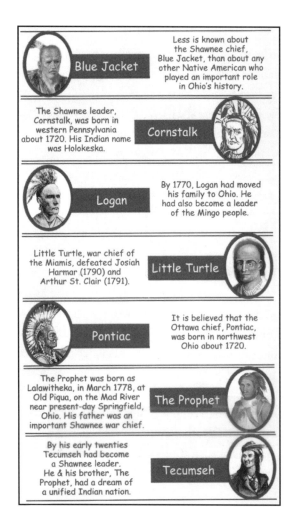

Blue Jacket — Less is known about the Shawnee chief, Blue Jacket, than about any other Native American who played an important role in Ohio's history.

Cornstalk — The Shawnee leader, Cornstalk, was born in western Pennsylvania about 1720. His Indian name was Holokeska.

Logan — By 1770, Logan had moved his family to Ohio. He had also become a leader of the Mingo people.

Little Turtle — Little Turtle, war chief of the Miamis, defeated Josiah Harmar (1790) and Arthur St. Clair (1791).

Pontiac — It is believed that the Ottawa chief, Pontiac, was born in northwest Ohio about 1720.

The Prophet — The Prophet was born as Lalawitheka, in March 1778, at Old Piqua, on the Mad River near present-day Springfield, Ohio. His father was an important Shawnee war chief.

Tecumseh — By his early twenties Tecumseh had become a Shawnee leader. He & his brother, The Prophet, had a dream of a unified Indian nation.

raids upon forts in the Great Lakes. The British retaliated. An English army marched into Ohio in 1764 in reaction to the conflicts spurred on by Pontiac. Eventually a negotiated truce ended the violence. However, after a peaceful interlude there ensued a series of murderous exchanges between whites and Indians on the western frontier. One of the more notorious incidents involved the murder of several family members of a Mingo Indian chief named Logan (Logan, Ohio) by whites. In response to this brutal killing, Logan combined forces with the Shawnee chief Cornstalk. 300 Indians attacked an army of Virginians in 1774. This was known as the Battle of Point Pleasant (Ohio). The Indians fought well, but ran short of ammunition and were forced to withdraw from the battlefield. The battle was the central conflict in a series of minor skirmishes between whites and Indians which became known as Lord Dunmore's Wars. Lord Dunmore was the colonial governor of Virginia at the time.[23]

The most significant battles between Ohio Indians and Americans took place under the combined leadership of Chief Little Turtle and Blue Jacket. By 1790 Little Turtle had gathered a large contingent of Miami Indians to live at a village on the forks of the Maumee River (Ft. Wayne, Indiana). Miamistown, as this new settlement was known, was linked to other older Miami villages present in the area. The Shawnee also lived nearby under the leadership of Blue Jacket. Furthermore, there were Delaware villages present in the immediate vicinity. This loose coalition of Indian settlements was a source of concern for American settlers spreading westward. The Americans recruited an army of 1,453 from Kentucky and Pennsylvania to address the growing Indian threat. The force was placed under the command of General Josiah Harmar. Harmar marched his men toward Miamistown in the fall of 1790. Faced with far superior numbers, Little Turtle and Blue Jacket launched a surprise attack upon the Americans. The Indians routed the large army near Ft. Wayne, Indiana. Josiah Harmar hastily called for a retreat of his forces. After this embarrassment, the Americans were determined to take care of the Indian problem. Secretary of War Henry Knox called for an army of 3,000 men to confront the Indians. The military force was to be under the leadership of Governor Arthur St. Clair. A little under 2,000 men were gathered in response to the challenge. The army marched to the west in 1792 to once again attempt to dispel the Miami and Shawnee Indians. Bad weather and desertion plagued St. Clair's army. The force was down to about 1,400 when it reached the Wabash River in western Ohio. In the meantime, the Indians had gathered and placed sole leadership of their forces under Little Turtle. 1,000 warriors came to Maumee Valley to meet this second American challenge. The Indians were rested, confident, and knew the terrain. Their plans were aided in part by a young Shawnee scout named Tecumseh who reported on the strength and movement of St. Clair's troops. Little Turtle attacked the unsuspecting troops of St. Clair as they camped on the Wabash River. The surprise was total. The Americans had a total of 918 casulties—623 soldiers killed and 258 wounded. The Indians lost only 21 warriors with an additional 40 wounded.[24] Little Turtle and Blue Jacket had managed to outwit and humiliate two large American armies. The Americans kept coming.

The outcome of the third round between the soldiers and Ohio Indians was to produce different results. This time President Washington appointed General Anthony Wayne (Mad Anthony) to command the legion. His men marched to the site of St. Clair's crushing defeat and erected a fort (Ft. Recovery, Ohio). The fort was a reminder to the army of its recent inglorious past and the seriousness of the task before them. The army paused to construct another fort in defiance of the Indian threat (Ft. Defiance, Ohio). By this time, Wayne was expecting an Indian attack at any moment. Little Turtle had sensed that the tide had turned

to the Americans and urged his followers to negotiate for peace. Blue Jacket felt otherwise. Blue Jacket assembled a force of 1,000 warriors to ambush Wayne about five miles from Fort Miami. Ft. Miami was a recently constructed British fort on the Maumee River. Blue Jacket assumed that if his warriors failed, they could retreat to the safety of the British fort. Anthony Wayne was ready for the Shawnee when they

attacked on August 20, 1794. The battle of Fallen Timbers was a short conflict lasting little more than an hour. Few casualties occurred on either side. The Shawnee attack was repulsed and the Indians were pushed back in retreat. They ran for the safety of Ft. Miami. The British, however, failed to open the gates of the fort to their fleeing comrades. The Indians were broken by this act of treachery. The defeat left

no option but to bargain for peace.

The Treaty of Greenville, signed in 1795 between Americans and Indians, fueled an influx of white settlers to southwestern Ohio. The treaty had provisions for land north of Greenville, Ohio, that would be reserved for the natives. Settlers would be welcome to live south of the treaty line. For the next fifteen years there would be relative peace between the Ohio Indians and Americans. The fate of the brilliant war chief Little Turtle was a cruel one. Following the Treaty of Greenville, Little Turtle felt that the survival of his people depended upon peaceful coexistence with the Americans. Accordingly, he adopted some of the white man's ways and visited with American Presidents. The Americans hailed him but treated him as a trophy won at war. His fellows Indians were critical of his accommodations to the white man. In the end, Little Turtle lost the respect of both friend and foe.[25] The life of Blue Jacket is fascinating in that it weaves together so much of the complex relationship that existed between Americans and Ohio Indians. Little is know about the early life of Blue Jacket. Because of this, historians are divided upon his background. Some historians have suggested that Blue Jacket was actually a white man. Duke Von Swearingen was a young white man who was taken into captivity by the Shawnee Indians in 1771. Von Swearingen became accustomed to Indian ways and rose to prominence as the war chief named "Blue Jacket."[26] If we are to accept this theory, then Blue Jacket had a brother who came to Highland County, Ohio. Joseph Von Swearingen was born in 1763 and served his country in the Revolutionary War. After the Revolution he married Nancy Evans. Joseph came to Highland County when the Evans family settled on Clear Creek in 1799. The Von Swearingen family dropped the "Von" from their name early on. There are many descendants of Joseph who live under the Swearingen name in Highland County in the present day. Joseph Swearingen emerged as Highland County's first Representative to the Ohio Legislature. He died in 1836 and was buried in Highland County.[27] However, the preponderance of historical evidence discounts the notion that Blue Jacket was a white man. Most historians place Blue Jacket as an Indian born into the Shawnee tribe in Pennsylvania somewhere around 1740. By 1772 he had become a war chief among the Shawnee of the upper Scioto River where he had a village on Deer Creek. His influence rested upon his ability as a warrior and connections and familiarity with whites.[28] The life of Blue Jacket is portrayed every summer in outdoor drama near Xenia, Ohio.

The decade after the Treaty of Greenville was a torturous one for Ohio Indians. Settlers continued to flock to their previous hunting grounds. There was widespread death due to epidemics. The animal population was dwindling. Liquor was becoming a way of dealing with depression. The Shawnee chief Tecumseh posed a solution to these problems. Tecumseh was born at Pickawillany

Greenville Treaty Line

(Piqua, Ohio) in 1768. The Miami Indians, before the coming of the Shawnee, had occupied the village. As a young man, Tecumseh witnessed the coming together of Europeans from different backgrounds to form a new nation (the United States). This experience gave him the dream of accomplishing a similar union among the Indians. Tecumseh desired for the various tribes to come together as one people. He traveled extensively from Minnesota to

Alabama and from New England to Kansas in preaching his message of Indian unification. Tecumseh had the kind of intelligence and dynamic personality which engendered respect. He was fluent in English. He was sharp enough to use the white man's religion to make his point. In one dramatic encounter with his main adversary (William Henry Harrison), he said: *How can we have confidence in the white people when Jesus Christ came upon the earth you kill'd and nail'd him on a cross, you thought he was dead but you were mistaken.* The parallel with the resurrection of Jesus and the forthcoming rising of the Indians was clear enough for Harrison to be concerned.[29] Tecumseh supplied the necessary charisma to energize a call for Indian solidarity. However, it was left to his brother, Tenskwatawa (the Prophet, also know as Lalawitheka), to fuel the movement with religious fervor. As a young man, the Prophet developed the ability to enter into a spiritual trance in which he received visions. These revelations formed a coherent plan of action for Native Americans. It was a call for a return to the old and avoidance of outsiders. The Prophet urged his followers to return to Indian rituals and the traditional lifestyle. He argued that the tribes had been contaminated by the influence of the Americans. There was to be no liquor permitted in this new Indian community. Dependence

AFTER THE SIGNING OF THE TREATY OF GREENVILLE, OHIO INDIANS AGREED TO STAY NORTH AND WEST OF THIS LINE. THIS ALLOWED WHITE SETTLERS TO POUR INTO SOUTHWEST OHIO WITHOUT THE THREAT OF INDIAN VIOLENCE.

upon European technology was prohibited. It was the customs of Indian ancestors that would govern as opposed to dictates from the Great White Father. For a people depressed and with little hope, this vision of Indian pride was empowering. In 1808 the dreams of Tecumseh and the Prophet began to bear fruit. The invitation went out for Indians of every tribe and from all persuasions to come live at a new village to be guided by Tecumseh and the Prophet. Hundreds of Native Americans responded to the challenge. Prophetstown (Lafayette, Indiana) was born out of an intense desire to regain Indian pride and respect. Prophetstown also gained the worried attention of the American government.

In 1800 the Congress of the United States divided the Northwest Territory into two parts. President Adams appointed William Henry Harrison as Governor of the new Indiana Territory. Governor Harrison kept a close watch over the growth and development of Prophetstown. In the fall of 1811, the timing seemed right for Harrison to make a military strike upon the Indian settlement. The feared Tecumseh was absent from Prophetstown. He was to the south visiting Indian tribes. His brother was left in charge of the village. The Prophet was a remarkable religious leader,

marched his army toward Tenskwatawa risked surprise attack. The managed to fight off the gain victory on November 7.

but he was not a military man. As Harrison marched his army toward Prophetstown, everything on a Americans Indian charge and gain victory on November 7. The Battle of Tippecanoe broke the Indian resistance and created a national hero out of William Henry Harrison. Harrison rode his fame all the way to the White House. He served for one month as President of the United States in 1841. The circumstances of his death are unusual. Harrison at age 68 was elected as President of the United States. He gave a long inaugural address (one hour and forty minutes) outside on a cold, winter day. He caught a cold which turned into pneumonia. He died one month later after serving in the office of President for one month.[30]

Tecumseh was destined to a tragic end. Tecumseh returned home shortly after the defeat at Tippecanoe. Prophetstown was all but a deserted village when Tecumseh arrived. With broken spirits, Tecumseh continued the fight. He joined the British with other Indian allies to fight the Americans in the War of 1812. He died at the October

1813 Battle of Thames in Canada. The life of Tecumseh is portrayed every summer in outdoor drama outside of Chillicothe, Ohio.

With the death of Tecumseh, the last serious Ohio Indian threat was removed for the Americans.[31] The Ohio Indians never stood a chance against the tide of the white man from the very beginning. The Europeans had overwhelming numbers, resources, and technology. There was one group of Europeans who had a markedly different approach to the Native Americans. The story of the Quakers and Indians is in contrast to the history of violence that took place between the white man and natives.

QUAKERS AND INDIANS

ONE OF THE MAIN THEOLOGICAL tenements of Friends is that "there is that of God within every person." This presupposition allowed Quakers to view the Native Americans as human beings with the same potential to discover the divine as himself or herself. There were other European groups who sought to bring the Christian religion to the Ohio Indians. The Moravian work among the Delaware Indians living in Northeast Ohio in the late 1700's is one strong example of the Christian faith as it was brought to bear on the frontier. The Europeans meant well when they attempted to share their faith with the natives. However, far too often the conversion of Indians turned out to be just one more way for the white man to force his world upon the original inhabitants of the land. There was no significant appreciation for the Indian culture and religious traditions. The Quakers who came to America did try to enter into and understand the Indian point of view. William Penn began his colony of Pennsylvania with religious tolerance and openness toward people of all races and creeds. Penn engaged in peaceful treaties with the natives, and at first Pennsylvania was largely free of the frontier violence which plagued other colonies. John Woolman carried on the same tradition of Penn in his visits to the Indians in the mid 1700's. In his Journal, Woolman writes about the motivation behind his journey to the Native Americans: *Love was the first motion, and thence a concern arose to spend some time with the Indians, that I might feel and understand their life and the spirit they live in, if haply I might receive some instruction from them, or they might be in any degree helped forward by my following the leadings of truth among them.*[32] Thomas Beals shared a similar concern for the Shawnee of the Ohio country when he visited in the late 1700's. Quakers and the Shawnee established friendly ties. In 1821 Quakers founded a school for Indians at Wapakoneta, Ohio. The

THE WALLS OF FORT ANCIENT LOCATED IN WARREN COUNTY, OHIO. MOST ANTHROPOLOGISTS BELIEVE THE SHAWNEE ARE DESCENDANTS OF THE FORT ANCIENT INDIAN CULTURE.

Friends taught Shawnee students the basics of English, writing, and arithmetic. They showed the boys how to plant and harvest while the girls were instructed upon the duties of housekeeping. The Quakers did not attempt to teach the Shawnees the principles of Christianity but gave them skills to live in the American world.[33] The Friends who came to Highland County aspired to live at peace with the Shawnee.

One incident is of particular note. In the spring of 1803, a Captain Herrod, who was a prominent settler living outside of Chillicothe, Ohio, was found tomahawked to death. His death was supposed to have been the work of local Indians. This theory was later disproved. However, the white settlers sought revenge for his death. The whites in turn took part in the murder of an innocent local Shawnee chief named Way-wil-a-way. It seemed that tensions between Indians and whites would escalate to the point of open warfare between the two groups. Several hundred Indians collected at the forks of Lees Creek in Highland County near Leesburg. Nathaniel Pope asked for a council to be held with the chiefs under the branches of a spreading elm (which stood for many years near Fairfield Meetinghouse). The Indians at this council suggested that a property settlement be made for the death of Chief Way-wil-a-way. The Indians wanted half of the settler's provisions and salt, plus all the blankets that could be found. A snag developed in the negotiations when Mrs. Pope stated her objections. Daniel Scott tells us, *The idea of parting with her blankets could not be endured by Mrs. Pope, so she flatly refused and the treaty was on the point of being broken off. One of the Indians then picked up her youngest son, then a lad of some ten or twelve years of age, and standing him up against a tree, went through the motions of tomahawking and scalping to show her what would be the consequence to the whole family of a persistence in her refusal. She not assenting promptly, he then stepped off fifteen or twenty feet and commenced throwing his tomahawk and sticking it in the tree a few inches above the boy's head, the surrounding Indians laughing loudly the while. This Mrs. Pope could not endure, so the treaty was ratified at once.*[34]

The Pope family had been pioneers, planters, and peacemakers in Highland County. The role of pilgrims was the final chapter to be played in the life of this Quaker family.

CURRENT ISSUES

THE SEPTEMBER 11, 2001, ATTACK upon America was conducted by terrorists. White settlers living on the Ohio frontier would consider Indian attacks as acts of terror. Terrorism and other acts of violence grow out of the ground of cultural misunderstandings and mistrust. The Indians and the white man came from two very different places. They found it difficult to appreciate each other. In the present day, nations in the Middle East and the United States come from two different cultural and religious traditions. These two regions of the world find it hard to have a healthy regard for one another. The building of world community requires breaking down the atmosphere of suspicion and hostility. Mutual respect will be achieved when we are able to enter into another's worldview. Security will be gained when we can turn an enemy into a friend.

The Quakers who came to Highland County demonstrated that it was possible to live at peace with the Indians. The sharing of a common humanity and the ability to view each other as created in the divine image forged the bonds of peace.

Sources—

1. Lewis Savage, *History of Friends Church in Leesburg, Ohio: A Glorious 150 Years: 1802–1952*, self-published manuscript, page 9

2. Albert Cook Myers, *William Penn's Own Account of the Lenni Lenape or Delaware Indians, Tercentenary Edition*, Middle Atlantic Press, Wilmington, Delaware, 1970, pages 41 & 42

3. *Newsweek*, September 10, 2001, cover story, *Mormons: A Changing–But Still Mysterious–Religion Gets Ready For Its Olympic Close-Up*, page 49

4. Tanya West Dean & W. David Speas, *Along the Ohio Trail: A Short History of Ohio Lands*, Auditor of State, Jim Petro, Columbus, Ohio, 2001, page 8

5. Violet Morgan, *Folklore of Highland County*, Greenfield Printing, Greenfield, Ohio, 1946, page 13

6. Allan W. Eckert, *That Dark and Bloody River*. Bantam Books, New York, New York,1995, page XX and 637

7. R. Douglas Hurt, *The Ohio Frontier: Crucible of the Old Northwest: 1820–1830*, Indiana University Press, Bloomington & Indianapolis, 1996, page 10

8. Dean & Speas, *ibid*, page 23

9. Eckert, *ibid*, page XLIII

10. Andrew R. L. Cayton, *Frontier Indian*, Indiana University Press, Bloomington & Indianapolis, 1996, page 33

11. Cayton, *ibid*, page 33

12. Dean & Spears, *ibid*, page 19

13. Daniel Scott, *History of the Early Settlement of Highland County, Ohio*, Southern Ohio Genealogical Society, Hillsboro, Ohio, 1890, page 90

14. Cayton, *ibid*, page 6

15. Hurt, *ibid*, page 30

16. Cayton, *ibid*, page 35

17. Dean & Spears, *ibid*, page 78

18. Cayton, *ibid*, page 15

19. Cayton, *ibid*, page 27

20. Cayton, *ibid*, page 73

21. Stephen Ambrose, Undaunted *Courage: Meriwether Lewis, Thomas Jefferson, and the Opening of the American West*, Touchstone Book published by Simon & Schuster, New York, New York, 1996, page 343

22. Scott, *ibid*, page 59

23. Cayton, *ibid*, page 81

24. Hurt, *ibid*, page 118

25. Cayton, *ibid*, pages 166, 204, 217 27. Elsie John Ayers, *Highland County Pioneer*

26. Elsie Johnson Ayers, *Highland County Pioneer Sketches & Family Genealogies*, Hammer Graphics, Inc., Piqua, Ohio, 1971, page 8

27. Ayers, *ibid*, page 13

28. John Sugden, *American National Biography, Vol. 3*, Oxford University Press, New York, Oxford, 1999, pages 64-66

29. Cayton, *ibid*, page 219

30. James B. Cash, *Unsung Heroes: Ohioans in the White House: A Modern Appraisal*, Orange Frazer Press, Wilmington, Ohio, 1998, page 14

31. Cayton, *ibid*, page 224

32. John Woolman, *The Journal of John Woolman and A Plea for the poor: The Spiritual Autobiography of the Great Colonial Quaker*, The Citadel Press, Secaucus, New Jersey, 1774, reprint 1972, page 142

33. Hurt, *ibid*, pages 364 & 365

34. Scott, *ibid*, page 79

CHAPTER FOUR

Pilgrims:

The Quakers were strong in their belief that there was direct divine revelation and communication given to every man, and religion therefore was primarily of individual conviction and experience. They held that there was no need for ritual in worship and that the practice of baptism and the Lord's Suppers was not essential. Women were given equal rights with men. War was held to be incompatible with the spirit of Christianity, and they refused to take oaths because all swearing had been forbidden by Christ.

–History of Friends Church in Leesburg, Ohio by Lewis Savage

LIVING ON THE OHIO FRONTIER required sacrifice. The white settlers who crossed over the Ohio River left behind family, friends, and conveniences. The threat of hostile Indians, contracting dreaded disease and an uncertain future awaited the Americans who came to Southwest Ohio in the late 1700's and early 1800's. One of the comforts in this new environment was the certainty of religious conviction. The Christian faith was to find a variety of expression in the Ohio Country. Denominations with strong Puritan roots would come to the new territory.

Sects and communal groups found a home in Ohio. The winds of revival sparked the creation of an entire new church in frontier Kentucky and its neighbor in Ohio. Friends were part of the pilgrims who came to the frontier.

The Quakers who came first to Leesburg in 1802 did so as part of a religious community. Friends came to an area not as individuals, but within the context of families and the Christian faith. It is instructive to note that Leesburg's founder was not a single person but instead three men (Nathaniel Pope, James Howard, and John

A TRADITIONAL MEETING FOR WORSHIP.

FRIENDS, IN THE
EARLY DAYS AT
FAIRFIELD,
WORSHIPPED WITH
MEN AND WOMEN
ON SEPARATE
SIDES. THE
SEPARATION OF
WOMEN LED TO THE
DEVELOPMENT OF
OUTSTANDING
FEMALE LEADERS
SUCH AS
BATHSHEBA
LUPTON—SEE THE
BEGINNING OF
CHAPTER THREE
FOR INFORMATION
ON BATHSHEBA
LUPTON.

Walters). The Meeting was the primary commitment which banded Quakers together as they traveled westward. The Meetinghouse was the focal point for Friends' community. Lewis Savage describes the typical Friend's Meetinghouse that was built on the Ohio frontier. This is the Fairfield Meetinghouse (Leesburg, Ohio) constructed in 1822–23 and it still stands today: *The long low rectangular building*

had plain glass windows and two doors, the one on the right for men, and the one on the left for women. The interior of the building was plain and was divided by a partition and sliding shutters into two equal parts. The shutters were left open for worship but were closed for their separate business meetings. The benches were plain and straight and set at floor level. At the front there was a raised platform with two or three facing seats for the use of ministers and elders. There was no pulpit, no organ, no pictures, no lamps, no ornaments to attract the eye and disturb the worship.[1] One has a picture in mind of a quiet community of faith living in a pastoral setting when describing Quakers.

In sharp contrast to the quiet Quakers was the birth of another religion. As the Friends migrated to Leesburg in 1802, a great religious revival was taking place south of the Ohio River. In northern Kentucky, the winds of Christian enthusiasm were shaking the frontier.

CANE RIDGE REVIVAL

A FEW MONTHS BEFORE HE DIED in 1820, Daniel Boone was asked if he had ever been lost in his many explorations. Boone is said to have replied, *"I can't say as ever I was lost, but I was bewildered once for three days."* [2] At age eighty-five, Daniel's humor was wry to the end. The experience of being "bewildered" was typical for American pioneers. It is hard for us to comprehend the isolation and the loneliness which confronted those who came to make a home on the frontier. Nowhere in the world were farmers scattered on their homesteads as they were in America. Thickets of forests and impassable streams separated various families. The danger of Indian raids made it a hazard to visit friends and relatives. The day was determined by the brief hours of sunlight. Night fall ushered in a canopy of darkness and a deep still upon the settlements nestled among the trees. Any remnants of the home left behind to the east were most welcome.

Religion became a primary source of consolation to the pioneer population. The little church resting in the wildwood became a symbol of that which was familiar and comforting to the pilgrims who came west. Attendance at church was a matter of social bonding and visiting with relatives as much as it was food for the soul. A visiting preacher would create quite a stir in any pioneer community. It was from this context that the great revival in Kentucky can be understood. The church historian John Boles tells us: *Often lodged in rude, isolated cabins, pioneer families sought through church membership to re-create what they most missed,* *the familiarity of old customs and beliefs... The poignant desire for community made many Kentuckians eager for revival.*[3]

James McGready was a Presbyterian minister who was the first to speak to this deep-seated need in frontier Kentucky. At the Gasper River Church in southwestern Kentucky, McGready introduced a primary feature of frontier religion. In July of 1800 Reverend McGready held a series of religious meetings which lasted for several days. The "camp meeting" brought settlers together for an extended period of time in a period of religious seeking. The genius of the camp meeting is that it allowed the lonely pioneers to establish social contacts as well as it placed their lives in the context of renewed Christian enthusiasm. The camp meeting was an immediate success and hundreds flocked to the gathering hosted by McGready.

One of the visitors to the McGready venture was a Presbyterian preacher who had recently been called to serve a church in Northern Kentucky. Barton Stone was deeply moved by the sincerity and conviction he observed in the faithful who came to Gasper River. He determined that he would make use of the methods used so effectively by McGready. In August of 1801, Barton Stone announced a series of meetings to be held at Cane Ridge Church where he served as pastor. No one could have imagined the

GROUPS OF
SETTLERS
GATHERED IN
SMALL CIRCLES AT
CANE RIDGE. THE
REVIVAL OFFERED
SOCIAL CONTACT AS
WELL AS SPIRITUAL
UPLIFT TO THE
LONELY PIONEERS.

immense crowd which would come to the meetings announced by Stone. When the great day arrived for the spiritual gatherings to commence, a throng of between ten to twenty-five thousand people appeared. This was at a time when near-by Lexington, the capital of the state, had a population of only two thousand.[4] The meetings at Cane Ridge lasted for a week and would have continued except

there were no provisions left to tend to the needs of the huge crowd. Not only were there large numbers of laypersons, but also a significant segment of clergy was present for the historic event. It is recorded that there were more than eighteen Presbyterian ministers with possibly a larger number of Methodist and Baptist preachers present. There were never-ending religious services and non-stop sermons held throughout the camp-grounds. Sydney Ahlstrom writes persuasively about the dynamics at work at Cane Ridge: *One must first try to re-create the scene: the milling crowds of hardened frontier farmers, tobacco-chewing, tough-spoken, notoriously profane, famous for their alcoholic thirst; their scarcely demure wives and large broods of children; the rough clearing, the rows of wagons and crude improvised tents with horses staked out behind; the*

gesticulating speaker on a rude platform... At night, when the forest's edge was lined by the flickering light of many campfires, the effect of apparent miracles would be heightened. For men and women accustomed to retiring and rising with the birds, these turbulent nights must have been especially awe-inspiring. And underlying every other conditioning circumstance was the immense loneliness of the frontier farmer's normal life and the exhilaration of participating in so large a social occasion.[5]

Critics of the Cane Ridge revival have dismissed it as a product of group psychology and excessive emotion. Yet, it is only through the lens of faith that a true understanding of the phenomenon of Cane Ridge can be ascertained. Pentecost had arrived upon the frontier. The Holy Spirit was ushering in a whole new manifestation of the power of God at Cane Ridge. We are indebted to Barton Stone for a description of the physical effect of God's presence at the revival. According to Stone, there were seven revival responses: the falling exercise, the rolling exercise, the "jerks," the barking exercise, the dancing exercise, the laughing exercise, and singing exercise. As the names suggest, an extreme physical reaction was often witnessed when individuals became convicted of their sinfulness.[6] God was not someone with whom to trifle. The Living Lord was on hand to transform lives.

The tremendous impact of Cane Ridge has been felt in many places. For one thing, the revival at Cane Ridge permanently rearranged the Protestant landscape in our nation. The Protestant church in Colonial America was dominated by denominations with strong Puritan roots. The Presbyterians, Congregationalists, and Episcopalians were at the forefront of religious life in the thirteen colonies. In the aftermath of Cane Ridge, those of the Methodist and Baptist persuasion ascended to large numbers in Protestant America. These two communions developed as the choice of faith for those spreading westward on the American frontier. The Puritan tradition had been replaced by faiths forged in the fire of revival. The Baptist and Methodist faith continue today as the largest Protestant denominations in our country. Furthermore, birth was given to an entirely new church at Cane Ridge.

Barton Stone had adopted theological viewpoints which were out of the mainstream of Presbyterian thought prior to the meetings at Cane Ridge. The revival pushed Stone further toward new thinking about the life and the purpose of the church. The Synod of Kentucky was skeptical of the teachings of Barton Stone and other leaders of the revival. The tension between the two factions climaxed when the Synod pursued charges against Richard McNemar who, along with Stone, was instrumental at Cane Ridge. The climax came in September of 1803 when the Presbyterian Synod voted to punish McNemar for his doctrinal stance. In response to this decision, McNemar, Stone, and four other Presbyterian ministers withdrew from the Synod to form an independent body. This new group urged the forsaking of all denominational loyalties and encouraged believers to simply call themselves "Christians." Stone and McNemar achieved immediate success with their preaching in north central Kentucky and southern Ohio. During the same time period, a father/son team was moving in the same theological currents as Barton Stone.

Thomas Campbell (1763–1854) was a Scotch-Irish Presbyterian minister who emigrated to Pennsylvania in 1807. Campbell was interested in the theme of Christian unity, as was Barton Stone. Campbell began preaching the doctrine of religion based upon the Bible alone and was met with enthusiasm by persons in the area of Washington, Pennsylvania. Soon Campbell felt at liberty to leave the Synod and form the "Christian Association of Washington". The turning point came with the arrival of his son Alexander Campbell (1788–1866) in 1809. The younger Campbell had the theological acumen and force of personality to give drive to this burgeoning new movement. Alexander Campbell shaped this return to primitive Christianity and shared it with frontier folk who were settling around the Ohio River basin. The Campbells were aided greatly in their ministry by the emergence of Walter Scott. Scott filtered the new teachings into a system of five points that could be easily described by using one hand. The "five-finger exercise" could be comprehended even by children on the frontier (faith, repentance, baptism, remission of sins, and the gift of the Holy Spirit). Scott made it a goal to witness one thousand people a year to be converted by the power of Christ with this plain-speaking plan of salvation.

Over the next fifteen years this version of Christian restoration was to speak to the hearts and minds of people moving north and south of the Ohio River. Followers of this new religion were now being called "Disciples of Christ." The Disciples of Christ were aware of their similarities to the Christian movement led by Barton Stone. The two groups merged their efforts in 1832 to form the Disciples of Christ Church. The Disciples were to experience tremendous growth in the 1800's. With a starting point of 22,000 converts in 1832, the church developed to 192,000 members by the time of the Civil War. In 1890 the denomination could boast of 7,246 churches with 641,051 members.[7]

The heritage of Stone, Campbell, and Scott is realized in our area today primarily through the Church of Christ. The Church of Christ remains true to its tradition of calling for unity in Christ and as such has no denominational headquarters. Each local church is considered independent although there is a loose affiliation to the larger body. Membership is strongest in the lower and eastern midwestern states and especially in Kentucky and southern Ohio. Recent estimates are that the Church of Christ is comprised of about 1,250,00 with 13,000 churches.[8]

The Christian Union Church is another branch on the Christian restoration tree which is important to southwest Ohio. This fellowship was organized in Columbus, Ohio, in 1864. There are currently 114 churches within this tradition. The majority of the churches are located in Ohio and total membership is 6,000. Highland County hosts the primary education institution for this communion. The Christian Union School of the Bible is located in Greenfield, Ohio.[9]

The Church of Christ in Christian Union separated from the Christian Union Church in 1909. The historic meeting took place at Marshall, Ohio. This heritage in general follows the lineage of Stone, Campbell, and Scott. There is also a strong influence of the holiness tradition mixed into the teachings. Circleville Bible College (Circleville, Ohio) trains ministers to serve the church. There is a total of 11,400 members in 260 churches.[10]

The little log meetinghouse at Cane Ridge stands today (Paris, Kentucky). It is open to the public for tours. The Cane Ridge revival remains a watershed in American church history. It marks the end of the colonial Puritan period and the beginning of frontier religion. A distinctive American religious heritage without European roots was home-grown at Cane Ridge. We leave the final word concerning this amazing revival to Barton Stone: *Many things transpired there, which were so much like miracles, that if they were not, they had the same effects as miracles on infidels and unbelievers; for many of them by these were convinced that Jesus was the Christ, and bowed in submission to him.*[11]

THE CAMP MEETING INAUGURATED by James McGready and popularized by Barton Stone came to be a vehicle of growth for the Methodist Church. The Presbyterians had initiated the camp meeting as a mechanism for revival. However, the theology and piety which was an outgrowth of Cane Ridge could not be absorbed by the Presbyterian structure. Revival seemed to mean division and strife for Synods. It was left to the fluid Methodist and Baptist fellowships to adapt their evangelism and beliefs to the revival mode. The Methodists had an eye for detail and planning. Prayer groups, ministers in various churches, and advertisement to the public were all set well in advance of the great meetings to be held. Attention was given to format in order to create a climax to be reached at a camp meeting. In many ways the camp meetings were the forerunner to the Billy Graham Crusades. Billy Graham has borrowed the system of extensive advance work in order to ensure the success of his crusade in a given city. The tent, the sawdust trail, and the altar became symbolic features of the camp meetings. The emphasis was upon the need for sinners to repent and become followers of Christ. Thousands responded to the invitation to receive Jesus as their Savior and Lord. At first the fire of evangelism burned brightly in the camp meeting tradition. However, after some time the meetings became formalized and were a social gathering as much as a tool of revival. Sydney Ahlstrom explains, *during the early nineteenth century the camp meeting was a great engine of Methodist expansion a very important part of the church's system... By the 1840s the original impulse was dying... Cabins and two-storied residence houses replaced the tents... In the later years the camp meeting became a resort, a place for an edifying vacation.*[12]

The phenomenon of rapid growth among Methodists in the first forty years of the nineteenth century is revealing. At the turn of the century, there were not more than sixty-five thousand Methodists in the country. Francis Asbury, the major leader of the movement in the United States, was experiencing serious health problems. Prospects for renewal did not look good. However, with the Cane Ridge revival and the fervor it spawned, the Methodist church exploded in growth. By 1812 circuits in the western territory had grown from nine to 69. In 1830 instead of one conference west of the Alleghenies, there were eight. By 1844 the Methodist faith had become the most numerous religious body in America with 1,068,525

members.[13] In the course of a single generation, the Methodist tradition had expanded from being a minor player on the American religious scene into becoming the dominant denomination in the nation. The camp meetings were just part of the reason for this success.

Perhaps a greater factor was the structure of the church which led to great flexibility. Methodists established circuits and charges for their clergy to tend to on the ever-widening American frontier. It was local people drawn from the rank and file of the west who became ministers. The ministers were educated and well-trained to meet the needs of the common folk. The Methodist structure was autocratic in that authority came from the top. Bishops were the central figures in the emerging western conferences. However, the actual ministry was always local in nature and great leeway was given for clergy to minister as they saw fit within the confines of their charge.

The greatest accomplishment of both the Methodist and Baptist fellowships is that they were suited to the needs of populations on the move. For the Baptist faith it was the farmer-preacher model which took precedence. As the settlers moved ever westward in search of land to farm, the Baptist religion expanded with them. Local Baptist congregations headed by preachers who were part of the

common masses were the key to understanding dynamic growth. For the Methodist tradition, the archetype became the circuit-riding preacher. The foundation of Methodist outreach was the clergy who ministered to isolated clusters of people gathered on the frontier. For a lonely population with minimal contact to the outside world, the coming of clergy on horseback would have been immensely exciting to frontier settlements. Paramount among the circuit riding preachers was Peter Cartwright (1785–1872). The life of Peter Cartwright is an intriguing mixture of religion, politics, and a glimpse of the Methodist church as it grew with the population.

Peter Cartwright was born in Amherst County, Virginia, in 1785. His life paralleled the Methodist church. When Peter came into the world, the Methodist Church was separating from the Episcopal Church to form its own communion. As the Methodist Church moved on the frontier, so did the Cartwright family. Peter Cartwright settled at Bourbon County, Kentucky, with his family when he was a child. As a youngster Peter became fond of dancing, fast horses, and gambling. When sixteen years old, he became so impressed with his mother's Methodist religion that he gave up his old way of life. Within four years of this change, Cartwright was a circuit-riding preacher assigned to the Scioto Circuit in Ohio.

The Scioto Circuit at the time included the entire area west of the river to Eagle Creek. The Scioto Circuit assignment of 1805–06 included Highland County. The formal beginning of the Methodist church in Highland County came when Peter Cartwright and James Quinn began visiting the home of James Fitzpatrick in 1805. Isaac Pavey also is credited as the founder of Methodism in Fairfield Township of Highland County with meetings being held at his home in 1805. We gain some sense of the origins of the church from a description from a family member who was present when James Quinn first came wandering through the wilderness to the Fitzpatrick home: *Quinn was the first preacher who ever came to our house. He came wandering along through the woods from George Richards' hunting our house, late one afternoon. We had nothing but a little bench for a table, but we got him supper. He remained all night, and sat up late talking and praying with us.*[14] Cartwright also made it a practice to stop at the Fitzpatrick home during that year.

Peter Cartwright was just twenty years old at the time of this appointment. We have a feel for the demands placed upon the frontier preachers by the rapidly expanding population when the records indicate that James Quinn had thirty-one appointments to travel to every four weeks.[15]

Cartwright continued as a minister in Ohio for a short time before following the pioneers to the west. Peter Cartwright ended up in Illinois following the Methodist circuit. As he traveled, he became an outspoken critic of the institution of slavery. Slavery was the burning issue which nineteenth century Americans could not avoid. Cartwright left Kentucky to minister in the Northwest Territory because it was free soil. Speaking on slavery would necessarily involve a minister in the politics of the time.

Peter Cartwright was a Democrat and later in his life decided to join the political fray by running for elected office. In 1846 he was the Democratic nominee for a congressional seat in Illinois. His opponent was a young man running on the Whig party platform. This young man was Abraham Lincoln. Cartwright was well-known and popular through his many years as a preacher. However, he proved to be ineffective as a political campaigner. As election day grew near, Cartwright realized that he trailed Lincoln. In a desperate measure to gain support, Cartwright launched the accusation that Lincoln was an infidel. Troubled by these charges, Lincoln responded by printing a handbill. In the handbill Abraham retorted: *Although it is true I am not a member of any Christian Church, my position is held by several of the Christian denominations...*

I could never support a man for office, whom I knew to be an open enemy of, and scoffer at, religion.[16] Lincoln need not to have worried. The voters of the Seventh District elected him to Congress by an unprecedented majority.

Disagreements among politicians often cool over the years. This proved to be so for Cartwright and Lincoln. In 1859 Peter Cartwright appeared in court as a key witness for the defense which Abraham Lincoln was heading as a lawyer in a celebrated trial.[17] Cartwright's enduring contributions were not in politics, but religion. He remains as a model of the Methodist circuit rider who was essential to frontier religion.

The United Methodist Church today bears the fruit of the Cane Ridge revival and the first generation which followed it. Today this communion boasts a membership of 91,124,575 members in 37,875 local churches.[18]

Shaker Heyday

THE CANE RIDGE REVIVAL GENERATED intense religious enthusiasm and expectations. Not only had Pentecost come, but the Millennial reign of Christ was being ushered in. This was fertile ground for the United Society of Believers in Christ's Second Coming (the Millennial Church). This group of believers was more commonly known as the Shakers. This fellowship had come to the American colonies from England in 1774. It arrived on the shores of the new world with eight followers and the leadership of Mother Ann Lee. Mother Ann had been converted to Christ under the ministry of Jane and James Wardley who were part of the Quaker movement. She was a woman of a rich interior spiritual life. Ann Lee was given to visions in which she saw the Second Coming of Christ arriving in the form of a woman. Her piety convinced her and others that she was that woman. Despite this unusual doctrine, the church developed and grew during the years of the American Revolution. The 1784 the death of Ann Lee did nothing to impede outreach by the sect. Other capable leaders took her place, and by 1794 there were twelve Shaker communities scattered throughout New England. The grounds for expansion were to come with the western revivals. The religious fervor created by the Cane Creek revival planted ideal conditions for the Shaker seed to take root. The Shakers believed that the millennium of Christ had begun with the appearance of Ann Lee who was Jesus incarnate. The miracles performed at Cane Ridge convinced many that Jesus was indeed at hand.

In the spring of 1805 the New York Shaker community

sent three missionaries to Northern Kentucky *to visit the subjects of revival, in that country, with a view to search out the state of their minds, and open the testimony of salvation to them.*[19] The emissaries came with the confidence and zeal of those who posses ultimate truth. They met with an audience hungry for signs and determined that the end times were near. It is little wonder that some of the leadership of the Cane Ridge revival would be converted to the Shaker message. Richard McNemar was the first major figure to respond to this call to radical Christian living. McNemar was a well-trained Princeton theologian who had been instrumental at the Cane Ridge revival and had led the movement to form an independent Synod in Kentucky. Matthew Houston, John Dunlavy, and John Rankin, were other important ministers of the time who quickly followed McNemar into the Shaker fold. The first Shaker community to be established in the west was Union Village in Lebanon, Ohio (1805). The missionaries extend

SHAKER SETTLEMENTS IN OHIO AND KENTUCKY FLOURISHED IN THE AFTERMATH OF THE CANE RIDGE REVIVAL.

their work to form Shaker villages at Eagle Creek and Straight Creek in Adams and Clermont Counties of Southern Ohio (1805). Watervliet, near Dayton, Ohio, (1806) and Pleasant Hill in Kentucky (1806) were the next to be established. South Union, Kentucky, (1807) and West Union, also called Busro, Indiana, (1807) soon followed. North Union and White Water, both in Ohio, were begun in 1822.[20]

It was not only the millennial expectations which attracted converts, it was also the emphasis upon hard work and community living. The Shaker communities were marvels of Yankee efficiency. Sydney Ahlstrom explains: *The clean-lined functional buildings, spotless interiors, gracefully practical furniture, wonderful cattle herds, fine herb gardens and perfectly tended fields all witnessed to organizational, social, and economic success.*[21] So successful were these spiritual communes that they sparked a wide-spread American interest in communal experiments during the first half of the nineteenth century.[22] The Shaker dance (from whence the name of the faith originates), the Shaker furniture, and the emphasis upon simplicity are all testimonies from this tradition which hold up well today. The current interest in organic food and living in harmony with nature also have strong Shaker roots. The Pleasant Hill Shaker community in Kentucky is of particular interest because of its restoration. Pleasant Hill (outside of Lexington, Kentucky) has been brought back to its original condition and is open to the public for tours and overnight guests.

The Shakers reached their peak membership in the first half of the 1800's. There were approximately 850 Shakers in Kentucky with a total national membership embracing 6,000.[23] The purchase of Shaker property in Clinton County, Ohio, in 1856 was one of the last outreaches in our area. It is revealing to note how the Shakers intended to bring people into this community: *Late in 1857 the Shakers made an intensive effort to meet their Clinton County neighbors by visiting in homes, participating in local seances, attending a quarterly meeting of the Martinsville Quakers, touring a nearby Catholic academy in Brown County, and holding a Shaker meeting at Westboro.*[24] There were no converts gained by this journey to Clinton County and the community never took off. This was typical of the Shaker experience after 1850. From 1850 and beyond the Shaker movement went into a slow decline with the result being that by the early twentieth century the tradition was nearly non-existent.

The response to the Shaker missionaries in the aftermath of the Cane Ridge revival was not uniform.

Barton Stone, in particular, was dismayed by the Shaker teachings. Stone was alarmed to view the attraction of McNemar and others to this heretical Christian doctrine. Furthermore, his dream of Christian unity was being threatened by yet another schism in the life of the church. Stone is just one of several who were concerned that Christians should adhere to orthodox faith. The life of John Rankin (separate from the John Rankin who joined the Shakers) demonstrates a minister of the time who was orthodox in faith but went on to play a pivotal role in the great social drama of nineteenth century America. John Rankin was a Presbyterian minister who began his career shortly after the western revivals. His ministry demonstrates important linkage between frontier religion and the social movements which were so vital to America in the 1800's.

John Rankin was born in 1793 in Jefferson County, Tennessee. He was deeply religious as a youth and prepared for a career in the ministry with training at Washington College. Dr. Samuel Doak, a Princeton graduate, had founded this Presbyterian school in Eastern Tennessee. Upon graduation in 1816, Rankin headed north with his wife whom he had met while a student at college. His first formal pastorate was the Concord Presbyterian Church in

THE RANKIN HOUSE SITS ON TOP OF A BLUFF OVERLOOKING THE OHIO RIVER AT RIPLEY, OHIO. JOHN RANKIN AIDED MORE THAN TWO THOUSAND ESCAPED SLAVES IN THIS HOUSE.

Northern Kentucky. This was one of the churches which Barton Stone had served as pastor during the Cane Ridge revivals. This was followed by a series of short term pastorates in Kentucky. The decisive moment came when Rankin and his family moved to Ripley, Ohio, in 1822.

The slavery question was tearing churches apart. Rankin chose to move across the Ohio River to minister upon free soil. In 1828 he built his house upon Liberty Hill overlooking the Ohio River. It was in this house that Rankin and his family, which was to include thirteen children, assisted 2,000 escaped slaves. For forty-five years Rankin served as pastor at two different Presbyterian churches in Ripley, Ohio. He also held revivals in churches throughout southern Ohio during this period. At the same time, Rankin was writing tracts and pamphlets and traveling to New England on behalf of the abolitionist movement. He had one foot planted in the evangelical tradition of the recent past as witnessed by the western revivals, and the other foot was planted in the emerging religious humanitarian movement as demonstrated by his ministry to slaves.[25]

The social and humanitarian outreach of Americans in the 1800's was often fueled by religious fervor. The God who called people to be concerned about the spiritual welfare of others also was interested in their social setting. The temperance movement, prison reform, better conditions for mental patients, and women's rights were causes which took root in our nation after the turn of the

UNCLE TOM'S CABIN STIRRED MANY PEOPLE TO JOIN THE ABOLITION MOVEMENT PRIOR TO THE AMERICAN CIVIL WAR. TWO OF THE PRIMARY CHARACTERS FROM THE BOOK WERE BASED UPON ACTUAL RUNAWAY SLAVES WHOM HARRIET BEECHER STOWE LEARNED ABOUT FROM JOHN RANKIN.

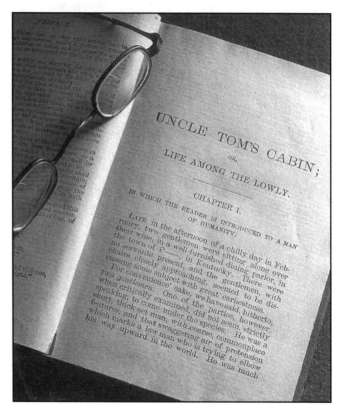

century. Fundamentally, they were broad based expressions of moral and social justice. The saving gospel heard at Cane Ridge was also necessary to be brought to bear around the world. Missionary societies in all denominations formed as a means to bring Jesus to every culture. The American Bible Society sprang up as a means to spread God's Word, the Sunday school movement began as a vehicle to train God's people, and church schools and seminaries were founded for the purpose of education for the Lord's ministers. Dwarfing everything else was the debate about slavery which engulfed the nation. To view every human being as being created in the divine image was the defining passion for abolitionists. The scriptures which John Rankin studied could lead him in no other direction than to be opposed to the institution of slavery.

A providential occasion for Rankin came with the visit of Harriet Beecher Stowe. Harriet Beecher was the daughter of a prominent minister who lived in near-by Cincinnati, Ohio. She, like Rankin, was a fervent abolitionist. She listened to the account told by Rankin of a slave who carried her child across the thawing ice of the Ohio River while her captors pursued her. This story became the dramatic highlight of a book she was writing, *Uncle Tom's Cabin*. The 1852 publication of this book was vital in stirring public opinion in our nation concerning the plight of slaves.[26] John Rankin continued to live in Ripley, Ohio, until after the Civil War. His house sits on a bluff overlooking the Ohio River and is open to the public for tours.

Quaker Pilgrimage

JOHN RANKIN WAS NOT ALONE in his efforts to aid escaping slaves. The most prominent worker in the southern Ohio abolitionist movement was Levi Coffin, a Quaker who had been active in aiding slaves escape while living with his family in Newport, (now Fountain City) Indiana. Levi Coffin continued this ministry when his family moved to Cincinnati, Ohio, in 1847. His endeavors on behalf of the slaves earned for Coffin the title, "President of the Underground Railroad." The 1876 publication of his book *Reminiscences* brought to life the stories of the slaves as they escaped during the pre-Civil War era. Levi Coffin was just one of a number of Quakers who assumed places of leadership in the social movements which fanned across America and England in the nineteenth century. Coffin was joined by Susan B. Anthony, Lucretia Mott, and John Greenleaf Whittier on this side of the Atlantic. In England, John Bright and Elizabeth Fry were Friends

faith. The Quaker belief in the equality of women and men lent itself to the development of female leadership. In addition, an emphasis upon direct revelation of God's spirit to every human being would necessitate the need to eradicate slavery and work for prison reform.

Lewis Savage outlines articles of faith for the Quakers who established Fairfield Meeting in Highland County: *The Quakers were strong in their belief that there was direct divine revelation and* who took leading roles in social movements.[27] For a religion which consisted of a small segment of the population, the Quakers carried a huge influence in the humanitarian and religious causes which were sweeping over Britain and the United States in the 1800's. Some of this rising forth among Friends can be explained in their assumptions of *communication given to every man, and religion therefore was primarily of individual conviction and experience. They held that there was no need for ritual in worship and that the practice of baptism and the Lord's Supper was not essential. Women were given equal rights with men. War was held to be incompatible with the spirit of Christianity, and they refused to take oaths because all swearing had been forbidden by Christ.*[28] The simple faith of a people being obedient to the "still small voice of God" is what is suggested by the Friends who first came to what is now Leesburg. These peaceable people constructed the Fairfield Meetinghouse in 1822-23. This house of worship stands today as a testimony to the practices of a venerable faith. There have been changes made to the building over the years. The changes reflect the transitions of a growing nation and the ways in which religion responded to new challenges.

By the end of the 1800's, there were major forces in technology and communication reshaping America. The railroad, the telegraph, the mass-circulation newspaper, and the development of urban centers were all forces in late nineteenth century America effecting major change. Quakers were no longer a peculiar people exempt from the advances of the world. James Baldwin illustrates the differences he discovered in his Quaker home town of Westfield, Indiana, in the 1840's and 1850's compared to the Quakers he found in Westfield when he returned in 1910: *The Westfield of the 1840s and 1850s was a place of women in dove-colored "plain" bonnets and men in broad-brimmed beaver hats and shadbelly coats... The inhabitants spoke of "thee" and "thine"... They worshiped in an utterly plain, barnlike building they called a meetinghouse. There the men and women sat separately, with the elders and "weighty" Friends facing them at the front.* In his 1910 visit to the Quakers in Westfield, Babbit was surprised to find: *They worshiped not in a meetinghouse but in a steepled church... An organ for music and a pulpit filled by an elegant minister replaced the facing benches. The plain language was a memory associated with long-dead grandparents, gone too were shadbelly coats and plain bonnets... The Quakers of Westfield were no longer separate from the world—they had become part of it.*[29]

Similar changes occurred to Friends who lived in Leesburg. In the 1890's remodeling was engaged at Fairfield Meetinghouse to accommodate the newer styles of worship. A pulpit was installed and a platform raised to assist a preacher. Separate doors for men and women were torn out to make room for single doors at the front and the back of the church. New windows and new brickwork was performed upon the meetinghouse. In effect, the Fairfield Meetinghouse had been rearranged to reflect the look of a mainline Protestant congregation. Currently, efforts are being enacted to restore Fairfield Meetinghouse back to its original condition. The building is the property of the Leesburg Friends Meeting. It remains the oldest church building in Highland County. Tours of the building can be arranged by contacting the author of this book. Donations toward the restoration efforts at Fairfield Meetinghouse would be gratefully received by the author.

The author would also enjoy talking about portions of this book to interested groups.

John Fitzgerald
149 South St., P.O. Box 393
Leesburg, OH 45135
(937) 780-9375
e-mail jfitzgerald@in-touch.net

POSTSCRIPT

AS FOR NATHANIEL POPE, he was a **pioneer** and one of the founders of Leesburg, Ohio. He was a **planter** in that he became a land owner and elected official in Highland County, Ohio. He was a **peacemaker** as witnessed in negotiating a treaty with the Shawnee. He was a **pilgrim** and continued to seek God in his Quaker Meeting.

CURRENT ISSUES

THE PSALMIST WROTE, *LORD, THOU HAS* been *our dwelling place in all generations... from everlasting to everlasting, thou art God.* (Psalm 90:1–2) The Almighty is eternal and without change. Yet, we are but mortal flesh and limited to a brief threescore and ten years upon earth. Therefore, each succeeding generation must discover God on its own terms. The first generation of white settlers who came to this area were pilgrims just as we are today. Several current Christian denominations can trace their spiritual roots to the frontier religion which originated in our part of the nation. Yet the influence of denominations has waned, and theologians suggest we are now living in a post-denominational era. The advent of new age religion and eastern religion has added to the melting pot of the Judeo-Christian heritage of America. Some would say that ultimate religious truth is found only in their own tradition. Others maintain that God can be found in all faiths. The task before us is the same as that of our spiritual ancestors. We must encounter the Divine in our own, unique fashion. The truth we have experienced, we must share with our world. We must have hope for the future and look for evidences of the holy wherever we find ourselves.

The Quakers who came to Highland County believed that the light of Christ Jesus shines in each individual heart. There is a continuing invitation for all of God's children to participate in the light. Worship is an opportunity to enter into that light which shall never be extinguished. The final word belongs to the Quaker, John Greenleaf Whittier:

The Quaker of Olden Time

The Quaker of the olden time!
How calm and firm and true,
Unspotted by its wrong and crime
He walked the dark earth through.

O Spirit of that early day,
So pure and strong and true,
Be with us in the narrow way
Our faithful fathers knew.

Give strength the evil to forsake,
The Cross of Truth to bear,
And love and reverent fear to make
Our daily lives a prayer!

Sources—

1. Lewis Savage, *History of Friends Church in Leesburg, Ohio: A Glorious 50 Years: 1802-1952*, self-published manuscript, pages 12 and 13

2. Michael A. Lofaro, *The Life and Adventures of Daniel Boone*, University of Kentucky Press, 1986, page 130.

3. John B. Boles, *Religion in Antebellum Kentucky*, University of Kentucky Press, 1995, page 26

4. Sydney E. Ahlstrom, *A Religious History of the American People: Volume 1*, Doubleday & Company, Inc., Image Books, Garden City, New York, 1975, page 525

5. Ahlstrom, *ibid*, page 526

6. Boles, *ibid*, page 27

7. Ahlstrom, *ibid*, page 548

8. Frank S. Mead, Revised by Samuel S. Hill, *New Ninth Edition: Handbook of Denominations in the United States*, Abingdon Press, Nashville, Tennessee, 1990, page 92

9. Mead & Hill, *ibid*, page 77

10. Mead & Hill, *ibid*, page 93

11. Ahlstrom, *ibid*, pages 525 and 526

12. Ahlstrom, *ibid*, pages 530 and 531

13. Ahlstrom, *ibid*, page 530

14. Daniel Scott, *History of the Early Settlement of Highland County, Ohio*, Southern Ohio Genealogical Society, Hillsboro, Ohio, 1890, pages 125 and 126

15. Scott, *ibid*, page 125

16. David Herbert Donald, *Lincoln*, Simon & Schuster, New York, New York, 1995, page 114

17. Donald, *ibid*, page 150

18. Mead & Hill, *ibid*, page 164

19. Boles, *ibid*, page 38

20. Martha Boice, Dale Covington, Richard Spence, *Maps of the Shaker West: A Journey of Discovery*, Knot Garden Press, Dayton, Ohio, 1997, page 1

21. Ahlstrom, *ibid*, page 596

22. Boles, *ibid*, page 40

23. Boles, *ibid*, pages 40 and 41

24. Boice, Covington, Spence, *ibid*, page 101

25. John Rankin, *Life of Rev. John Rankin*, self-published manuscript, 1872, page 35

26. Owen Findsen, *Cincinnati: Then and Now: Ripley scene of Eliza's Escape*, printed in *Cincinnati Enquirer* newspaper, February 26, 1995, G 4

27. Hugh Barbour, *Slavery and Theology: Writings of Seven Quaker Reformers, 1800-1870*, Print Press, Dublin, Indiana, 1985, Introduction

28. Savage, *ibid*, page 12

29. Thomas D. Hamm, *The Transformation of American Quakerism: Orthodox Friends, 1800-1907*, The Indiana University Press, Bloomington & Indianapolis, 1988, page xiii